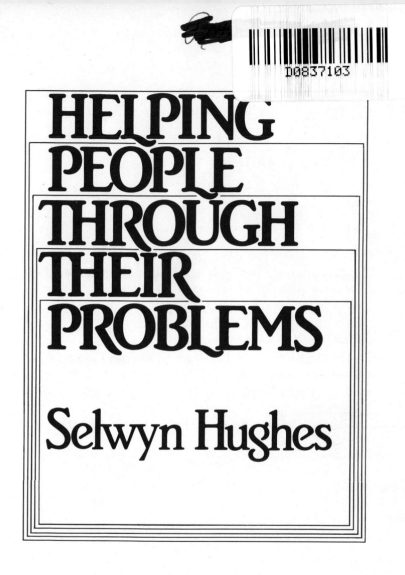

HELPING PEOPLE THROUGH THEIR PROBLEMS

Selwyn Hughes

BETHANY HOUSE PUBLISHERS
Minneapolis, Minnesota 55438
A Division of Bethany Fellowship, Inc.

Unless otherwise indicated, scripture quotations are taken from the King James Version of the Bible.

RSV=Revised Standard Version, copyright 1946, 1952 © 1971, 1973 by the Division of Christian Education of the National Council of the Churches of Christ.

PHILLIPS=The New Testament in Modern English, translated by J. B. Phillips, © J. B. Phillips 1958, 1960, 1972

TLB=The Living Bible, © Tyndale House Publishers 1971

Published in Great Britain under the title, *A Friend in Need*

Helping People Through Their Problems
Selwyn Hughes

Library of Congress Catalog Card Number 81-70198

ISBN 0-87123-201-4

Published by Bethany House Publishers
A Division of Bethany Fellowship, Inc.
6820 Auto Club Road, Minneapolis, Minnesota 55438

Printed in the United States of America

CONTENTS

**Other helpful books concerning
Christian counseling issues from
Bethany House Publishers:**

PREFACE

Early in my ministry an unkempt and distressed stranger came into my church vestry one night and asked for my help. He shared with me a deep, personal problem; but, having had no counsellor training in the theological college I had attended, and certainly having no innate abilities at helping people resolve their problems, I was able only to say, 'I will pray for you'—which I did. The next morning they fished his body out of the local canal. He had been dead, they said, for at least eight hours. After hearing the news I knelt on the floor of my study and, from the depth of my grief, cried: 'Lord, make me a counsellor.' From that day to this I have striven, by every means possible, to develop counselling skills and to address people at the point of their need.

I am convinced that helping people with their problems is not just the work of ministers and trained counsellors, but the task of *every* Christian, no matter at what stage he or she may be in the Christian life. Obviously there will be various levels at which we are all best able to help. Lawrence J. Crabb, in his book *Effective Biblical Counselling*, claims that there are three levels of Christian counselling: (1) counselling by encouragement; (2) counselling by exhortation; and (3) counselling by enlightenment. This book is aimed at helping people on the first two levels. Some problems are too deep to be dealt with by untrained laymen (Level 3) and these must be referred to those who have the wisdom and insight to handle them. Ideas and suggestions on how to help people at Level 3 will have to be the subject of a further book.

In this book I have tried, as far as possible, to avoid the awesome term 'counsellor'. A word I prefer is 'people-helper'. It has its limitations, of course, but it suggests a ministry in which every Christian can engage. That, I believe, is the message of the New Testament, and certainly the import of this book.

There can be no doubt that one of the greatest issues in the contemporary Christian church is the need to teach Christians how to bring the church to the level God has always wanted it to reach—that of a loving, caring fellowship. In some ways this is more important than evangelism, as there is nothing more appealing to an uncaring, non-Christian society than to see a community give itself in selfless service to others.

One of the major purposes of the Body of Christ is to help people with their problems. Christians are repeatedly instructed to demonstrate love in all their relationships. Some years ago, Harvard psychologist Gordon Allport called love 'incomparably the greatest psychotherapeutic agent in the universe'. He added that the Christian church knows more about this than anyone in today's secular society, but he regretted the 'age-long failure of religion to turn doctrine into practice'. If the love of God were to flow through us as it should and reach out to others, then the results would be staggering.

But to love is risky. It takes time and effort and involves us, sometimes, in a good deal of inconvenience. This is why we tend to talk a lot about love, but do very little to demonstrate it. This book is aimed at identifying the principles by which you can turn theory into practice and become a people-helper in the fullest sense of the word.

Our model is none other than the God of the universe. He has gone to the utmost length to demonstrate his love. So must we!

SELWYN HUGHES

1

WHAT ON EARTH IS THE CHURCH DOING FOR HEAVEN'S SAKE?

JOHN sat in church eagerly waiting for the Sunday morning sermon to begin. He was particularly expectant that day as, after a distressing week at the office, he was hopeful of receiving from God a word that would meet his personal need. John's work as a computer operator demanded a good deal of preciseness and exactness, but on the previous Tuesday he had made an error in his work which had cost his company a considerable sum of money. Naturally his employer had been deeply upset and on Friday he had called John into his office for a reprimand that was given in no uncertain terms. It was not so much the reprimand, but the way it had been given that hurt. John, a Christian for ten years, found that he was unable to rid himself of bitterness and resentment towards his employer.

He leaned forward as the pastor announced his text. Would the text give some indication of how he could solve his problem? No, nothing in *that*. He listened attentively as the pastor proceeded to probe the context. No, nothing in *that*, either. When the pastor was fifteen minutes into his sermon John leaned back in his seat, realizing that there was little hope of receiving instruction from this morning's sermon on how to handle his feelings of bitterness and resentment.

He glanced around. Other people seemed to be getting something out of the sermon, and he could see by the expressions on their faces that some of their needs were being met. As the sermon drew towards its close John mused to himself, 'This is a great sermon, but how I wish someone would help me with my problem.'

ANITA, a few seats away from John, had a problem of a different sort. A nurse at the local hospital, she had been obliged by reason of staff shortages to put in five consecutive weeks of night duty. And now she was feeling frustrated and depressed. Trying hard to suppress her negative feelings and concentrate on the sermon, she found it an impossible task, and settled back in her seat to focus on what was happening to her emotions. 'Is my depression chemically caused,' she thought, 'or is it being triggered by my anger and frustration?' Anita realized, instinctively, that her problem would largely be resolved if she could talk it over with a sensitive and sympathetic listener. Emotional release often follows the ventilating of a problem with an understanding friend. But who? Most of the congregation looked upon Anita as a self-sufficient, self-confident person, with few personal problems. 'If only,' she thought, '...if only they would let me slip out from behind my mask sometimes and accept me as I am—a frightened, insecure little girl.'

BRIAN, a fine-looking young man sitting on the back seat of the church, had an equally pressing problem. He had become a Christian a few months before and, although many of his old sinful habits had dropped away, he was still fighting a battle with impure thoughts. Lustful images rose, unbidden, into his mind. Would the pastor have something to say about this in his morning sermon? He had been helped before through something said from the pulpit; would some word come to him today that would help bring to a stop the merry-go-round of erotic images that filled his mind? As nothing being said from the pulpit seemed to meet his need Brian let his thoughts wander. There's Mr Kent...he looks a fine Christian...I wonder does he have a problem conquering impure thoughts? What would happen if I spoke to him about my problem? Would he be embarrassed?...Would he have nothing more to do with me?...Perhaps *real* Christians don't have this kind of problem...?

'*And now let us sing our final hymn.*' The announcement brought John, Anita and Brian back to the service and they stood to their feet along with the rest of the congregation. Although they were somewhat uplifted by God's presence in the service, each was deeply conscious that inside him rumbled deep personal needs that had not been met.

Once the benediction was over the congregation dispersed into the aisles to greet each other with the usual Sunday morning clichés. 'How are you?' 'Oh, I'm fine, thanks. How are you?' 'I'm fine, too, thank you very much.'

Anita hesitated as someone came up to her and said, 'How are you today, Anita?' She longed, desperately, to share with someone her real feelings; could this be the opportunity she was looking for? Unfortunately it was all too obvious, from the expression and tone of the questioner, that the greeting was no more than a cliché. Responding on the same level, Anita replied, 'I'm fine, thank you' and quickly walked away.

John and Brian dodged their way through the congregation without anyone engaging them in conversation—something they were grateful for, as neither of them wanted to be caught up in idle and meaningless chit-chat. An hour later, as John, Anita and Brian reflected on the morning service in the seclusion of their own homes, their one conclusion was, 'It was indeed a wonderful service, but how I wish something had been said that could help me with my problem.'

Is what I have described in the preceding paragraphs a mere caricature, or is it a down-to-earth representation of what goes on in most of today's churches? I'm afraid that all too often the picture I have drawn is of grim reality. The Christian church seems unable to minister to people at the point of their needs. It is not, as someone put it, 'scratching where people itch.' Both in the pulpit and in the pew the church is failing in its role as a loving, caring society.

Problem in our pulpits

'How,' we might ask, 'is the church failing in its pulpit ministry?' Pulpit sermons (with notable exceptions, of course) fail to touch the nerve of human need and grapple with the important issues of daily living. The church is strong on exhortation, but weak on explanation. The result is that in thousands of Christian congregations there are people like John, Anita and Brian who say to themselves 'This is a great sermon, but how I wish someone would say something that would help me with my problem.'

This point was brought home to me rather dramatically early in my ministry when, after delivering what I thought was a well-prepared and well-thought-out sermon, a man tackled me later in the vestry and said, 'I though that was a great sermon—now tell me how I can put it into operation in my life.' Ever since then I've tried to include the 'how' in almost every sermon I have preached. Isn't this where the church is missing the mark? We tend to answer the questions people are not asking, and countless numbers sit in our congregations saying to themselves, 'I know *what* I should do, but *how* do I do it?'

But this is not the only aspect of the church's failure in its pulpit ministry. Another mistake we make is to assume that all the problems related to Christian living can be answered through pulpit preaching. This is not to degrade pulpit preaching, or to attempt to render it valueless. It is a God-honoured and important way of teaching, instructing and inspiring the people of God, but it has one drawback—it fails to minister to people's *specific* needs. This can best be done when we talk to them *individually*. 'Every person,' says Dr Clyde Narramore, 'has his own interesting world. And we do not enter people's worlds by taking a pot-shot at them. We help people most when we talk to them on a one-to-one basis.' The church must stop thinking that once something has been said from the pulpit it is enough. If people's personal problems are to be solved, then pulpit preaching must be followed up by giving more individual attention to the issues. People do not grow or change much unless they are given an opportunity to discuss their problems thoroughly. To try to solve all problems through pulpit preaching is like trying to put drops into someone's eyes from an eye dropper held at a height of fifty feet!

Games Christians play

We said earlier that both in the pulpit and in the pew, the church is failing in its role as a loving, caring society. How is it failing in the pew? Even the most casual observer of church life today can see that in the area of inter-personal relationships things are not as they ought to be. It is perhaps the greatest scandal of the universe that a church modelled on a God who cared enough for us to give his own Son to die on a cross, should be so bereft of tender, loving care.

Take an average Christian congregation. People meet together in church on Sundays but rarely make any serious attempt to communicate with each other on a meaningful level. Colin Urquhart, when interviewed once on television, described such people as 'billiard-ball Christians'.

He went on to explain that in many churches, the only contact people have with each other is through well-worn clichés that have no real depth or meaning; they bounce these off each other like billiard balls going click, click, click. Then they settle back in their pockets for another week until they are brought out the next Sunday to begin the game all over again. This is contact without communication. There is no sensitivity to each other's needs, no alertness to hidden problems, and no desire to relate on a meaningful level.

Lawrence Crabb, a Christian psychologist, says, 'We warmly shake hands with people every Sunday who are about to come apart at the seams, and very often we don't know it until they really do.' Clearly this is far from the model of the church described in the Bible.

According to the New Testament, every believer is expected to have a practical and sacrificial concern for the needs of his or her fellow human beings. The apostle James asks us, 'Now what use is it, my brothers, for a man to say he "has faith" if his actions do not correspond with it?' (James 2:14, PHILLIPS). A similar thought is expressed by the apostle Paul in Philippians 2:4: 'Don't just think about your own affairs, but be interested in others, too, and in what they are doing' (TLB). Again, in 1 Thessalonians 5:11, Paul tells us to 'encourage each other and build each other up' (TLB), and in Galatians 6:2 he bids us to 'Share each other's troubles and problems, and so obey our Lord's command' (TLB).

Everyone a people-helper

Helping people with their problems is the responsibility of every Christian believer, no matter at what stage of spiritual development he or she may be. Baron Von Heugel, a Roman Catholic layman, gave this penetrating definition of a Christian: 'A Christian is one who cares.'

Every local church must accept the responsibility for helping people with their problems. The Bible fairly bulges with the truth that once we have opened up our lives to Jesus Christ and are invaded by his love, then our next task is to allow that love to flow out to others in ways that demonstrate a practical, sacrificial concern. We are 'to rejoice with those who rejoice, weep with those who weep' (Romans 12:15 RSV). We are to 'build one another up, admonish one another, encourage the faint hearted, help the weak, and be patient with everyone we meet' (see 1 Thessalonians 5:14). clearly then, we Christians must be sensitive to each others' needs and, wherever necessary, reach out to help.

As a young man I sat one Sunday in my local church with a deep spiritual problem I could not resolve. I looked to the pulpit for help but none came. As I was leaving the service, feeling somewhat sad and dejected, a young man tapped me on the shoulder and said, 'Can I have a word with you for a moment?' Never, as long as I live, will I forget the impact he made on me as he said, 'I couldn't help noticing that something is bothering you. I am not a counsellor, and I have no great experience in helping people with their problems. But I can promise you one thing—I am a good listener, and *I care!*' Those last two words were just what I needed. Within minutes I had shared with him the problem that was concerning me and, although he was unable to fully unravel it and resolve it, yet I left that service feeling as if I were walking on air. All because someone cared!

It is surprising what help one person can be to another when there is a genuine demonstration of tender, loving care. Some years ago psychologist, Robert Carkhuff, did a detailed study on the effectiveness of what is known as 'lay helpers'. His conclusions were quite startling. When lay helpers, with or without training, were compared with professionally-trained counsellors, it was discovered that 'the patients of lay counsellors did as well as, or better than, the patients of professional counsellors'. A number of reasons were suggested for this discovery.

> In contrast to a professionally trained person, a lay helper (a) is closer to the one being helped, knows him as a friend, and is thus better able to understand his problem, and to pick up non-verbal clues, or to demonstrate a sincere sympathy; (b) is more often available; (c) knows more about the helpee's family, work situation, life-style, beliefs, or neighbourhood, and can, therefore, take a more active part in guiding decisions, or helping the person change; (d) is able to communicate in language which the person can easily understand; and (e) is more down-to-earth, relaxed, informal, and inclined to introduce a tension-relieving humour.

Very often a trained counsellor or professional counsellor is attempting to work in accordance with some complex counselling theory. A lay helper couldn't care less about this. Since he is primarily concerned about another human being who is hurting, all his efforts are directed towards that end. He often ends up doing a better job than his highly-trained professional counterpart.

Specific God-given ability

Now at this stage someone might be saying to himself, 'Isn't the ability to help someone in trouble a special spiritual gift? And isn't it true that only some people are given this special ability?' Yes, some people are specifically gifted by God for the purpose of helping people with their problems, as outlined in Romans 12:6-8: '... and if our gift be the stimulating of the faith of others let us set ourselves to it' (PHILLIPS). The gift of 'stimulating the faith of others' is, in my opinion, the God-given ability to uncover and resolve the deep, hidden problems which hinder Christians in their spiritual growth. I witnessed this gift at work quite recently in a small group of Christians who had gathered to increase their effectiveness as lay helpers. One of the members of the group indicated that he had a problem in his life which he really couldn't get to the bottom of; he explained that others had tried to help him but, up to that moment, there had been no success.

A woman who had received no professional training in counselling and was in the group, as she put it 'to become a better people-helper', began to lock into his problem. Within minutes she had gently, and sensitively, traced the surface problem down to its root cause and brought the man face to face with the real issue. It was then a comparatively easy matter to set about resolving the problem. Time and time again, involved as I am in training and working with people to help them become more effective in helping people with their problems, I have been amazed at this wonderful gift which appears in certain people in the Body of Christ. I am thankful to God that he has put this gift into the midst of his people.

But if you do not have this gift, it does not mean that you have no responsibility for helping someone with their problems. In fact, the absence of any of these seven basic gifts mentioned in Romans 12:6-8 does not excuse us from fulfilling other scriptural commands. If, for example, a person does not feel he has the gift of 'giving' as described in Romans 12:8, this does not mean that he is exempted from supporting the work of God with his finances. Jesus said 'Give, and it shall be given unto you' (Luke 6:38). Similarly, if a Christian does not possess the gift of 'sympathy', he is still expected to show mercy and comfort to the weak (1 Thessalonians 5:14). This may raise the question, 'If we are all expected to do these things, then why the need for specific gifts?' The best answer I can give to this is to liken the church to a football team. Although some players have a specific function, all are expected to try to score goals. God has gifted people in specific ways in his church, but the absence of a particular spiritual gift does not exempt us from focusing our attention on our overall spiritual responsibilities. We may not all have a gift for counselling, but we are all expected to share Christ's love with each other and to demonstrate to the world that the Christian church is a loving, caring society.

If every Christian functioned in the way God expected, by showing a genuine love and concern for each other, then what a different view the world would get of the Christian church! 'Every generation must wage its own theological battles,' says Professor Howard G. Hendricks, 'but the sediment of the muddy waters of this generation settles into the issue of the doctrine of the Church.' I believe that as we move towards the close of the twentieth century, the Holy Spirit is seeking to focus our gaze on what Christ expects of his church and what kind of people he expects us to be. A good question to ask ourselves is this: is the world rejecting the church Christ designed, or the one we have degraded? Perhaps because we have offered them a caricature of the real thing, they are really rejecting the wrong item.

'The church,' said one preacher, 'is a great idea—if it wasn't for the people in it.' Likening the church to Noah's Ark, he went on to say, 'If it wasn't for the storm on the outside, we wouldn't be able to stand the stench on the inside.'

One of the major purposes of the church is to help people with their problems. 'God has so composed the body... that there should be no division in the body, but that the members should have the same care for one another. And if one member suffers, all the members suffer with it; if one member is honored, all the members rejoice with it. Now you are Christ's body, and individually members of it' (1 Corinthians 12:24-27, New American Standard Bible). J. W. Drane, in an article in *Christianity Today* entitled 'Fellowship—our Humpty

Dumpty Approach', says: 'In the fellowship that Christians have with one another, God wants to create a loving community that will be a witness to the non-Christian world... We can give the world conclusive proof of God's operation in our lives if our fellowship together is marked by that loving, sharing quality which is markedly absent in the world at large.' We don't need to look long and hard to know that the Body of Christ is not performing as it should. To be a true, helping community, as we are meant to be, we must return to the biblical pattern of every member committing himself or herself to the task of being a person of care and concern.

'Life,' says Dr E. Stanley Jones, 'is sensitivity.' The lower life is sensitive only to itself. The higher in the scale of existence you go the wider the range of sensitivity, and the deeper the depth. When you come to the highest life—that of Jesus—you find complete sensitivity. 'You can tell,' Dr Jones claims, 'how high you have risen in the scale of life by asking one question: How widely do I care, and how deeply?' All this, as we have seen, is based on a God who cares. The God we see in the face of Jesus Christ is a God who cares—cares enough to give himself on a cross.

What happens if we fail to reach out and help people with their problems? We become inextricably involved with ourselves and our problems. And every self-centred person is an unhappy person, with no exceptions. The person who says 'I couldn't care less about others' has to care more—distressingly more—about himself.

So the next time you go to church, or meet someone who is hurting, make this your prayer: 'Lord, make me sensitive, without being intrusive. Teach me what to say, and how to say it. And if I can't say much, then help me at least to care.'

'A Christian is one who cares.'

2
MAKING FOR THE GOAL

In order to effectively help people with their problems, one must have a clear goal. Objectives determine outcomes; we accomplish only that for which we aim. The great philosopher Aristotle once said, 'Like archers, we shall stand a far greater chance of hitting the target if we can see it.' A goal is like a car's headlights which throw a beam of light on the road ahead, giving clarity and direction to the driver. If when seeking to help people with their problems we have no clear road, then both we and the people we are trying to help may finish up in the ditch as casualties of the helping process.

A goal is a clearly identifiable target or objective. Without this we do not really help people—we hinder. If we don't know where we are going, then *any* road will get us there. David J. Schwartz, in his book *The Magic of Thinking Big*, stresses the importance of having clear goals in every aspect of life. He says, 'A goal is more than a hazy wish....It is a clear "This is what I am working towards."' When we lose sight of a goal we tend to concentrate on actions—like the pilot who announced to his passengers, 'I'm afraid we are lost; but cheer up, wherever we are going we are making good time.'

If a goal is so important, then what should be the chief aim of Christians who want to improve their effectiveness in helping other people with their problems? Is it the stopping of their tears? Is it the release of inner tension? Is it the recovery of a lost happiness? No. All these things may be an important part of the overall purpose, but the chief goal when ministering to weak and wounded brothers and sisters in the Body of Christ, is *to help them to become more like Jesus.*

After all, is this not *God's* chief goal for his children? Paul, writing to the church in Rome, said, 'For from the very beginning God decided that those who came to him—and all along he knew who would—should become like his Son' (Romans 8:29 TLB).

It was Paul's goal, too. Writing to the church in Colossae, he said, 'We warn everyone we meet, and we teach everyone we can, all that we know about him, so that, if possible, we may bring every man up to his full maturity in Christ Jesus. This is what I am working at all the time, with all the strength God gives me' (Colossians 1:28-29 PHILLIPS).

In order to bring this aspect of setting a clear goal more fully into focus, let's take a typical problem that could arise any time in your own Christian community. One evening after church someone approaches you and says, 'I wonder, can you help me? I know I am a Christian, but somehow over the past few weeks I seem to have lost the happiness I used to have. I read my Bible regularly, pray every day, and attend church as often as I am able. But nothing I do seems to help. I feel so frustrated and discouraged. Can you help me to be happy once again?'

Now your ability to help at this point will depend on a number of things—your understanding of Scripture, your experience, your willingness to listen, your ability to empathize, and your skill at asking questions. But what-ever direction you take in helping this person with his problem, the single most important factor will be how you see your goal. If you see it as merely helping the person to recover his lost happiness, then most of the encounter will be taken up with suggestions as to how to achieve that end. You might try to reassure the person that God still loves him and, providing he keeps reading the Bible, prays every day and attends as many church services as possible, the problem will eventually go away. This approach may well be supportive, but it is unproductive. Unless your primary goal is to help a person become like Jesus Christ, you are going to be trapped into dealing with surface symptoms rather than uncovering the basic causes.

Someone might ask, at this point, 'Is there anything wrong with wanting to feel happy?' Of course not. But a preoccupation with happiness often obscures the path to what the Bible describes as *joy*. Dr Lawrence J. Crabb, a Christian psychologist, says, 'The Lord has told us that there are pleasures forever at His right hand. If we desire those pleasures we must learn what it means to be "at God's right hand" (Ephesians 1:20). If I am to experience true happiness I must desire above all else to become more like the Lord, to live in subjection to the Father's will as He did.'

If we understand the Scripture rightly, the goal of Christian living is not happiness, but holiness. When we make it our responsibility to abide at God's right hand and live the way he designed us to, then he will make it his responsibility to flood our beings with his eternal joy. Happiness, as the word suggests, depends on what happens. Joy is independent of events. It keeps on flowing in the most dismal and depressing circumstances.

Most people, when facing serious problems, usually complain about their troubled feelings. They say such things as 'I feel so unhappy'; 'I get upset so easily'; 'I have gone past the point of feeling anything'. Take Frank, for example. Frank came to the Counselling Centre and began to share his problem with me in these words: 'I don't know what's gone wrong with my Christian life, but

I just don't seem to be getting as much out of it as I once did. I feel frustrated, and sometimes in church I feel like getting up and going out. I feel a hypocrite going on like this. Christians are supposed to be happy and the way I am at the moment, I am no advert for Christianity—at work or in my home.'

After discussing his problem a little more deeply, I asked him, 'Tell me, Frank, what do you expect to get out of your visits to the Christian Counselling Centre?' He thought for a few moments and said, 'I'd like to be happy again, to be able to sing the hymns and choruses in church and really mean it.' I responded to Frank's statement by saying, 'I'm glad God has given us the opportunity to be able to talk together about your problems. Something is obviously hindering the flow of God's power and peace in your life. As we open ourselves to him and to his Holy Spirit, I have no doubt he will show us what it is and enable you to recover the happiness you once knew.' During the hours of in-depth counselling that followed, Frank shared with me that he was involved from time to time in homosexual practice with a non-Christian friend. As we focused on this problem, Frank came to see that there was no way he could maintain a feeling of happiness or joy in his spirit while living in direct contradiction to God's word. When he confessed his sin, agreed to put this matter behind him, and took God's strength and power as his defence against future temptations, then, and only then, did his joy return and peace flood into his soul.

Frank is typical of many Christians whose feelings are disturbed because of some inner disharmony that has been brought about through a violation of one or more of God's principles. But, I hasten to add, not everyone who manifests disturbed or negative feelings does so because of a clash with God's commandments. Sometimes unpleasant feelings, such as anxiety, apprehension, insecurity and even depression, can come about through a serious deprivation of love during a person's childhood. If a child has not experienced unconditional love during his developmental years he can, when he reaches adult life, begin to show symptoms of this deprivation by experiencing the feelings I have just described. These feelings are not the result of some direct sin, but the consequences of a faulty parent-child relationship. If we seriously want to help people with their problems then we must be aware of this fact, and not jump to conclusions that a person's disturbed feelings are *always* the result of some violation of God's word.

I have found it useful, in my own attempts at helping people with their problems, to hold as an axiom that all disturbed feelings are a symptom and not a cause. My goal is to discover what is causing them and to remove the hindrance, and by so doing to help the person become more like Jesus Christ. If the hindrance is sin, then it can be dealt with by confession and repentance. If it is rooted in an unhappy experience or combination of experiences in the growing-up years, then it can be resolved by sharing the insights which are contained in God's word, the Bible.

We must be extremely careful when making it our goal to help people become like Jesus Christ, not to ignore their present distress and push them too quickly towards that goal. This is a mistake I made in the early days of my counselling ministry. Once I discovered that God's goal for his children was not happiness but holiness, then I decided to share this insight with the next person who came to me for help. A few days later a lady came into the counselling room and shared with me her problem in similar words to this: 'I am deeply unhappy in my marriage, and also in my church. I can find no satisfaction in either. My friends think that everything is fine, but no one knows how desperately unhappy I am deep down in my heart. Can you help me?' This was the moment I had been waiting for. Sitting back in my chair, with hands crossed in a typical philosophical pose, I said, 'Do you know that God is more interested in making you holy than happy?' I was stunned by the deafening silence that met this brilliant insight. A look of blank astonishment came over the poor woman's face, and from that moment onwards she couldn't get out of the counselling room fast enough! What was my mistake? I had imposed on her my goal of helping her to become like Jesus Christ, while ignoring her hurt and disturbed feelings. Her goal was 'How can I get rid of these unhappy feelings?' My goal was 'How can I help you to become like Jesus Christ?' But in attempting to move her towards my goal I had insensitively forgotten to relate to her in her present distress, and had too quickly confronted her with the reality of the situation. What she needed was a little sympathetic support, and then she would have been better prepared for the moment of confrontation.

For many years now I have been intrigued by this fact— that people, when seeking help or spiritual counselling, more often than not present their problems in the form of hurt feelings. 'I am unhappy.' 'I am frustrated.' 'I am so angry about this.' 'I am deeply hurt.' In all the years I have been working in the field of Christian counselling, I have never once had anyone come to me and say, 'I have a deep and pressing problem which is causing me a good deal of unhappiness. Will you help me solve it, so that I can become more like the Lord Jesus Christ?' The reason for this, of course, is that distress and difficulty push us towards a mood of self-preoccupation. John Powell, in his book *Why Am I Afraid to Love?*, tells how he once grappled with this problem. It was answered by a psychiatrist friend in these words: 'Did you ever have a toothache? Of whom were you thinking during the distress of your toothache?' John Powell says, 'His point was clear. When we are in pain, even if it be only the passing discomforts of an aching tooth, *we are thinking about ourselves.*'

There is nothing like pain, whether it be physical or psychological, to drive us inwards upon ourselves. When our feelings are hurt or upset, we tend to forget our commitment to a biblical life-style and concentrate on how we can relieve the symptoms, without much concern for the cause. Before we judge others and attempt to push them too hastily to the goal of becoming like Jesus Christ, we ought to stop and consider how we ourselves react when hurt.

A few weeks before commencing work on this book, my wife and I had the opportunity to enjoy a two-week holiday in the United States. For years we had dreamed of touring the six states of New England, and after landing at Boston we hired a car and set off on the journey. After several days of pleasurable driving, one morning we were lost. I stopped the car at the side of the road and started to check the road map, when suddenly a large and heavily-loaded lorry, coming from the opposite direction, swerved and slammed right into me. There was no personal injury, but the damage to the car was quite extensive. At that moment it started to rain very heavily, which added to the difficulties of the situation.

My immediate response to this situation was a mixture of anger, frustration and apprehension. I was angry at the lorry driver for not driving more carefully. I was frustrated because I could envisage the quick arrival of the police, answering questions, filling in forms, and the consequent hold-up to our holiday. And I was apprehensive as to what the outcome of all this would be. Here I was on an American highway, caught up in a situation which I might easily have avoided. Had I stopped earlier for a cup of tea when my wife suggested it, I would not have been at this point when the lorry came across the road. I found myself building up a strong hostility towards the driver of the offending lorry, and at that point there came into my mind the words of Scripture (a scripture which, by the way, I have often used when counselling others)—'When all kinds of trials and temptations crowd into your lives, my brothers, don't resent them as intruders, but welcome them as friends.' (James 1:2 PHILLIPS).

I thought to myself, 'a lorry slamming into the side of my car—a friend?' As we say, if this is a friend, then who needs enemies? As I sat and waited for the police to arrive to fill in the necessary accident forms, it occurred to me that the Sovereign and Almighty God who had saved me could easily have prevented this accident, had he wished. I knew that, according to Romans 8:28-29, God loves me and takes the most intense interest in the smallest detail of my life; he does not allow anything to happen to me unless it can be linked into his purposes to make me more like his Son, Jesus Christ.

As I began to consider these basic scriptural facts, a surprising thing happened. My feelings began to change. I began to realize that this lorry, lodged in the side of my hired car, could only be seen as a 'friend' if I stopped having self-centred goals, like going through life avoiding any hold-ups, difficulties, or mishaps. My musings in the fifteen minutes that I waited for the police to arrive began to clarify something which, although I had believed it for many years, I had not seen as clearly as I did at that moment. Whenever I fail to see anything that happens to me as a 'friend', according to James 1:2, then it is more than likely that my goal, at that moment, is a million miles from the mark of becoming like Jesus Christ.

My anger stemmed from the fact that my goals were self-determined. I was focusing at that moment on what was happening to me, rather than on how God could use this to deepen my character and make me more like Jesus Christ. The more I considered the facts of Scripture, however, the more I found that my disturbed feelings subsided and a sense of calm and peace spread through my whole being. Driving away from that scene after it was all over, I asked myself: 'What have I learned?' This was my conclusion: the next time I counsel someone who is hurt, angry, upset, or frustrated, then I will remember my own experience on the highway in Maine and try to minister to them with greater empathy and tender loving care.

It should be becoming quite clear by now that the goal of helping people with their problems is to move them from self-centredness to Christ-centredness. I am aware that this cuts right across the mood of this modern age. The current emphasis on self-expression, personal wholeness, and self for its own sake is a long way from the biblical goal of becoming like Christ. Unfortunately, many Christians have fallen into this trap of emphasizing self-expression as being the solution to many personal problems. For a while this works, but it exhausts itself very quickly. The soil of self was never intended to be the seedbed of eternal values. In all the years I have worked as a minister and a Christian counsellor I have never yet met a happy self-centred person. The self-centred are the unhappy and the frustrated. They express themselves, but then they don't like the self they express!

We must become aware of the depth of selfishness and self-centredness to which a person can descend when confronted by human problems. These problems can produce disturbing inner feelings from which the person seeks immediate relief. In our attempts to be supportive and to ease the burden, it is so easy to move a person towards a non-biblical goal. This is why we must keep in mind, continually, that our ultimate goal in helping people with their problems is to enable them to become like Jesus Christ. If, in the interests of a person's feelings, this biblical goal is set aside and the happiness of the person becomes supreme, then our counselling has descended to a secular level. We must do all we can to be supportive, reduce tension, ease the burden, and help people cope with the pressure of disturbed feelings, but not at the expense of failing to help them become like Jesus Christ.

Non-Christian therapists, psychiatrists and counsellors, with much of their thinking rooted in humanistic presuppositions, regard man's happiness and welfare as supreme. The ultimate goal then for such counsellors is to help people feel good. A. Lazarus, in his book *Behavior Therapy and Beyond* (McGraw Hill) says, 'You are entitled to do, think and feel whatsoever you please, provided no one gets harmed in the process.' This view, one shared by the majority of non-Christian counsellors, reveals the sharp division that exists between the Christian and the non-Christian approach to personal problems.

Ingrid and Anthony, a young Christian couple I once counselled, shared with me how wrong advice given by a non-Christian counsellor brought them to the verge of divorce. Anthony, a serviceman stationed in Germany, met and married Ingrid in an evangelical church in the town of Hamburg. After a few years of marriage they both began to drift away from Christ and it was not long before their relationship with him, and with each other, became lukewarm and then cold. In order to save their marriage, they visited a non-Christian psychiatrist who suggested to them that they might each consider engaging in an extra-marital affair. At first they were shocked with the suggestion, but the more they thought about it the more the idea appealed to them. Within a few months both of them were involved in sexual affairs outside their marriage, and their relationship seemed destined to end in divorce. Just about this time Anthony was directed by the army to a period of service in Northern Ireland. While spending a few weeks in England before taking up his duties, both he and Ingrid came to see me at the Counselling Centre. They told me the whole story and, although it took many hours of delicate handling and in-depth counselling, they both repented of their sin, claimed God's forgiveness and renewed their marriage vows to each other in my presence. Secular counsellors, because they do not work from a biblical base, seek to help a person achieve whatever that person feels will make him happy. The Bible says, 'There is a way which seemeth right unto a man, but the end thereof are the ways of death' (Proverbs 14:12).

Christian counsellors desire the happiness and welfare of the people they attempt to help too, but not in a way that violates biblical principles. A Christian, when called upon to help a person in trouble, will not be willing to help that person feel good in a way which contradicts biblical standards. One Christian counsellor I know tells how he was approached by a woman whose husband had left her. She was deeply distraught and after supporting her for a little while and showing a genuine concern for her predicament, he said, 'I want to go back to something you said a few minutes ago. You said that you would do anything to get your husband back. Is that really so?' 'Yes,' she said. 'I mean it. I would do simply anything to see him walk in that door.' The counsellor said, 'For example, would you lie to bring him back?' 'Yes,' she said 'If that is what it would take to bring him back to me than I would lie—much as it goes against the grain to do so.' Gently and lovingly, the counsellor then faced her with the reality of what she was saying. Her goal in this situation was the relief of her feelings. Understandable, of course, but it was not the biblical direction for her life—and, as a good counsellor, it was necessary for him to point this out. When she finally saw that she was seeking a solution to her problems along the line of self-determined goals, she asked God to help her bring her desires in line with his—the goal of becoming more like Jesus Christ. She found, as so many find when confronted with this issue, that when we decide to follow God's goals, then he takes care of our feelings and provides us not merely with a degree of happiness but with a joy that supports us in the very centre of the problem. As, by an act of will, we firmly decide to follow God's goals and devote all our energies to the task of becoming like his Son, then he fills us with a joy unspeakable and a peace which surpasses anything the world knows.

As potential people-helpers, each one of us must know and understand this truth, not merely in our heads but in our hearts. So the next time you face a personal problem ask yourself this question: 'Why do I want to solve this problem?' If the honest answer is so that you can experience feelings of happiness, then you are off target. Learn to swing your spiritual focus on to a more biblical goal. Say to yourself, 'I want to solve this problem in a way that will make me more like Jesus Christ.' If you can understand this truth, accept it, and absorb it into your spiritual life—then, and only then, can you transmit the truth to others.

If you really want to be successful at helping people with their problems, then you must face the fact that God will allow you to go through many personal difficulties so that you can develop a deep sensitivity to the feelings and problems which other people face. One counsellor said to me, 'Since I decided to become a Christian counsellor, I seem to have faced more troubles, difficulties and problems than I could ever have imagined!' I pointed out to him that one reason why God allows us to go through deep water is that he wants us to obtain a sensitivity which can then be used in the comfort of others. The Bible puts it like this: 'For he gives us comfort in our trials so that we in turn may be able to give the same sort of strong sympathy to others in theirs' (2 Corinthians 1:4 PHILLIPS).

Hold this truth continually before you and it will put a new perspective on all your problems.

3

WHAT YOU NEED TO KNOW ABOUT OTHER PEOPLE IN ORDER TO HELP THEM

Worriers, perfectionists, compulsive talkers, workaholics, overeaters, recluses... I am sure these 'types' can be found in your circle of friends just as they can in mine. And the study of their behaviour is intriguing. A friend of mine says, 'I've been fascinated with people ever since I came across them.' No two people are the same and, although they may sometimes behave in strange and unpredictable ways, as one Christian psychologist puts it, 'every person is worth understanding.'

Even in the Christian church some people's behaviour is difficult to understand. Why, for example, does Beryl become so devastated by even the slightest criticism? Why is John unable to handle a close relationship? What makes Fiona invariably take the opposite view to everyone else in her group? Human behaviour is not the result of a chance occurrence. There are reasons why people behave the way they do. Behind the attitudes and actions of our friends and acquaintances there is a history of experience which determines their behaviour.

Dr Clyde Narramore, a well-known writer and Christian counsellor, says, 'All behaviour is caused—and the causes are multiple.' Keep this statement in mind as you read through this chapter. It can become a significant key with which you can unlock the mysteries and complexities of human behaviour.

In order to understand 'what makes people tick', we must pause to examine the way God has made us. 'No person can understand why he behaves as he does,' says Dr James Mallory, 'nor the importance and implications of his behaviour, until he understands who and what he is.' The psalmist said that we are 'fearfully and wonderfully made' (Psalm 139:14). Paul, writing to the Christians in Thessalonica, said, 'And the very God of peace sanctify you wholly; and I pray God your whole spirit and soul and body be preserved blameless unto the coming of our Lord Jesus Christ' (1 Thessalonians 5:23). According to the Bible, each one of us has three parts to his being—a spirit, a soul, and a body.

The spirit is that part of us which is able to relate to God, communicate with him, and draw from him the motivation we need to run our lives according to his purpose. The soul is that part of us which contains the thoughts, the feelings and the decisions; or if you prefer, the intellect, the emotions and the will. Our physical body is the house which contains these spiritual and soulish faculties, and through the five physical senses—seeing, hearing, feeling, tasting and smelling—our inner being makes contact with the physical world around.

Although the diagram overleaf shows spirit, soul and body in separate compartments, it must be understood that this is for explanation purposes only. Human behaviour does not occur in isolation; these areas overlap and interrelate. For example, when a person suffers physical pain it will not be long before his emotions are affected. And when his emotions are affected it won't be long (unless preventive measures are taken) before his spirit is affected. Conversely, when a Christian is out of touch with the Lord in his spirit, then it won't be long before his soul is affected, and what affects the soul can also affect the body. In order to help people effectively and to understand why they behave and act the way they do, we must keep this fact very firmly in mind.

GOD'S DESIGN IN MAN

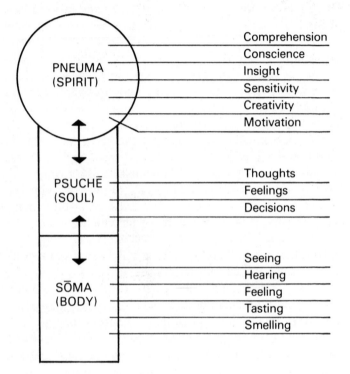

	Comprehension
PNEUMA (SPIRIT)	Conscience
	Insight
	Sensitivity
	Creativity
	Motivation
PSUCHĒ (SOUL)	Thoughts
	Feelings
	Decisions
SŌMA (BODY)	Seeing
	Hearing
	Feeling
	Tasting
	Smelling

If we say to someone who is suffering from a serious physical or emotional problem, 'Go home and read your Bible,' then we are simply displaying our ignorance of the fact that a person is made up of three distinct and separate parts. We are not recognizing the whole person. Similarly, if we attempt to solve a person's emotional problem by focusing exclusively on the spiritual, we will not get very far. The same thing applies if we try to treat a person's spiritual problems as if it were an emotional one. One of the first tasks in helping a person cope with problem behaviour is to try to determine the basic cause. Is it due to a physical disturbance or malfunction in the body's chemistry? Is it due to an emotional factor with its roots in some childhood experience? Is it a spiritual problem arising out of his lack of communication with the Lord? Or is it a combination of all three?

In order to put this whole matter more fully into perspective, let's bring each area of our beings into clear focus.

Physical factors

It might seem an unnecessary statement to make, but nevertheless I am going to make it—*everyone has a body*. I haven't seen anyone without one, have you? And no body functions perfectly. Due to Adam and Eve's violation of God's purposes for their lives in the garden of Eden, every human being born into this world is subject to sickness, disease and infirmity. Some of these physical problems arise from inherited predispositions to certain sicknesses; others from injuries, accidents, climate, lack of vitamins, or environmental factors. Sometimes a physical problem, such as glandular imbalance or neurological impairment, may give symptoms which to an inexperienced person appear to be emotional or spiritual difficulties. It is important to recognize this; otherwise you might find yourself trying to help a person with what appears to be an emotional or spiritual problem, but which is really rooted in a physical disharmony or disturbance.

A few years ago a lady wrote to me concerning her five-year-old child who, she said, was 'extremely hyperactive'. Her concern for the child had led her to seek help from a healing evangelist who told her that the child was 'demon possessed' and needed deliverance from the demon spirits that indwelt him. Upon receiving her letter, I immediately wrote back cautioning her about accepting this diagnosis until she had explored other areas, and suggested that she took the child to a doctor for a complete physical examination. She did just that, and wrote back a few weeks later to say that the doctor had diagnosed a small degree of brain damage in the child and that treatment had been started, with already some encouraging results. We kept in correspondence, and after a few months the mother told me that the situation was well under control. Although there were occasionally a few problems, the child was, to all intents and purposes, pursuing a normal life and making considerable achievements at school. Imagine the serious psychological damage that would have been done to that child had he been taken to a service of exorcism, prayed over, and supposed evil spirits cast out.

Having made many mistakes in the early part of my own counselling ministry, I have come to recognize the importance of encouraging a person to have a complete medical check-up before permitting him to go through a series of in-depth counselling sessions. It was brought home to me most forcibly when a friend of mine, Brian, came to see me over what he described as 'a serious spiritual problem'.

Brian had always impressed me as an outstanding Christian. His charming personality and many talents secured for him an ever-widening circle of friends. But, for some reason, he seemed to have lost his spiritual motivation. He said he no longer wanted to read his Bible, pray, witness, or go to church. I spent several weeks with Brian trying to diagnose his problem, all to no avail. There appeared to be no sin in his life, just spiritual lethargy and indolence. Casually, one day, I suggested to Brian that he might consider getting a thorough medical check-up. At first he didn't seem to regard the idea as important, but eventually he did. On his way home from the doctor he dropped in to see me, to tell me the news that his physician had diagnosed a condition known as hypoglycemia. This is a condition which can cause a marked change in a person's mood and personality, and is basically due to a malfunction of the body's mechanism which regulates and controls blood sugar levels. It is quite easy to regulate, and after a few weeks of medication and treatment Brian was his old self again. I could have attempted to have counselled him for months, with no significant progress, if I had not hit on the idea of sending him for a medical check-up. Since then, whenever I am confronted with someone who appears to require a few weeks of counselling, I request them to first obtain a thorough medical examination. Over and over again I have seen the value of this. If there are physical problems and they are not corrected, then weeks of spiritual and emotional counselling will be of little avail.

Having seen that physical factors greatly influence and affect human behaviour and attitudes, let's turn our attention to the second of these causative factors.

Psychological factors

Man is much more than a physical being with needs for food, water, air, light and warmth. He is a personal being and, as such, has personal needs. And unless these personal needs are met he will not function adequately as a person. Over and over again when talking to someone who is depressed or downcast, you will hear the heart-breaking lament, 'I just don't feel like a person.' Though the physical needs may well be met there is an inner emptiness, a deadness and a deep discontent which some attempt to palliate by over-indulging their physical needs to the point of gluttony.

In order to help people effectively at the point where

they are hurting, we must learn to clearly identify their basic psychological needs. Most psychological problems —such as depression, anxiety, irrational fears, uncontrolled temper, sexual problems, chronic lying, sudden mood swings—are the result of a person trying to cope with unmet personal needs. If basic personal needs are not properly met in childhood, then when the child becomes an adult he will sometimes develop a pattern of behaviour which, unknown to himself, is really a direct or defensive attempt to try and meet those basic needs.

What then are these basic psychological needs? Some psychologists produce a list of twenty to thirty basic needs, but really they can all be narrowed down to three: (1) the need to belong, (2) the need for self-worth, and (3) the need to achieve.

Every person needs the assurance that he belongs—that he is desired, wanted, and that in his absence he is missed. The search for a feeling of belonging motivates much of human behaviour. It begins to make itself evident from the moment of birth. We begin life as a tiny, helpless infant, under the care of loving (or otherwise) parents. Our parents have the sovereign power of giving or withholding, loving or not loving, hurting or helping. During the first year of our lives the need to belong is very dominant. If, for whatever reason, our parents failed to minister to that need—failed to feed us, comfort us, love us, kiss us, cuddle us, and make us feel that we belong—then this deprivation causes some cracks to appear in the foundation of our existence. The negative impressions we gain, such as 'I am not certain that mother will meet my needs' or 'why do I have to go into a rage before someone gives me attention,' can, if they are regular and consistent, form an impression about life which we carry into adulthood.

A child whose basic need to belong has not been properly met will, more often than not, develop deep anxiety and an inability to trust. Jean was like this. In a counselling session she said, 'Why am I so anxious about everything—and why do I find it difficult to trust? I can't trust my husband, my children, my friends; and I find it difficult to even trust God.' I said, 'Tell me about your childhood. Did you have any parental problems?' 'What's that got to do with it?' she countered. I pressed her gently until she told me a story I have heard so often before, of being unwanted, uncared for and unloved. When I explained to Jean that what she thought was a spiritual problem was really rooted in her early impressions about life, gained from a deprived childhood, the enlightenment she found motivated her to work with me towards the solution. 'If my behaviour was caused in that way,' she concluded, 'then it can be changed.' 'I couldn't agree more,' I said, 'so let's start working on ways to change it.' The way in which we worked together to change those early impressions will be the subject of a later chapter. But just to give you a little glimpse of the direction we followed, let me quote from the notes of an address which Jean gave to her church group on the subject, 'What God Showed Me in a Counselling Session.'

Some people go through life never being able to trust anyone—even God himself. They have a deep anxiety about everything and carry a gloom and pessimism with them everywhere they go. I was one of them. God showed me that if our basic needs are not met in childhood, then this can produce cracks in the foundation of our lives. Later, when we build the house of life on that foundation, the cracks widen and the house shifts. Family responsibilities, choosing a career, physical illness, and many other things produce such a pressure on these foundations that it becomes difficult to cope. I thought my problems were spiritual, but I came to see that they were really emotional and rooted in these early deprived relationships. God solved my problem by helping me to get rid of the bitterness and resentment I was carrying towards my parents for not giving me the love they should, and then showing me that no matter what has happened in the past, he was willing to be to me a Father and a Mother who would never fail. As I meditated on this fact it gave me a new foundation to my life and I discovered the most thrilling insight I have ever known—that what was caused, can be changed through the power of his everlasting and eternal word.

Although it is not always recognized, a reflection of the early impressions we receive in life is seen in adult behaviour and conversation. A wife said tearfully to her husband during a counselling session, 'You do things without my knowing, and it makes me feel as if I don't belong to you. I feel angry, upset and rejected by this, and I have no way of coping with it.' As we talked, I discovered that she had never had her need to belong fully met in childhood, and the hurt she was getting from her husband's behaviour was made more acute by this situation. When she learned how to bring this unmet need before the Lord and to let him be her comfort, her husband's actions, though unchanged, did not hurt her in one tenth of the way they did before.

So keep in mind that the unmet need to belong may often be responsible for a person's actions and behaviour.

Every person needs to feel a sense of personal worth and to feel valued—not so much for what he does, as for what he is. As we grow a little older, beyond the first year of life, a second basic need becomes prominent—the need for self-worth. If, for example, our parents (due to their own imperfections and lack of understanding) failed to convince us that we were loved by them irrespective of the way we behaved, then this impression would most certainly have a negative effect on our self-image. We develop our self-image in accordance with our parents' impression of us. If when we looked into their eyes we saw the attitude, 'I love you only when you behave well, do well in school, or come up to my standards,' then we tend to form a picture of ourselves as valuable not so much for what we are, as for what we do.

It is this impression which drives people to become workaholics—those addicted to work. They are never comfortable with themselves unless they are always achieving, always performing and always doing better than someone else. They cannot conceive that they can be loved for what they are as people, and thus they knock themselves out to gain attention through what they do.

Psychologists have long observed that if a child is not sure of his parents' love, then he will settle for the next best thing—attention. The way in which he attempts to get this attention will differ from child to child. With some it will be achievement, with others it will be rebellion. When such children come to adulthood they will go through life seeing their value more in what they do than in what they are—unless they have matured enough to understand what has been happening to them and take the steps to correct it.

It was this that prompted Elsie, the young wife of a Methodist minister in the west country, to drive all the way up to London to see me. 'My husband,' she said tearfully, 'is going to have a breakdown, because he is doing far too much—much more than he can comfortably handle.' He had already told his wife that he would not go to anyone for counselling, so there was very little I could do under the circumstances. As we talked, I heard again the old familiar pattern of a man who, when he was a child, was told by his parents, 'If you do good we will love you and respect you.' Believing his worth to be in what he did, he threw himself into everything he did in the hope that he would gain his parents' love and approval. Now, as a young minister, he had changed his parents for his church. He saw his congregation as people who would not approve of him unless he was working himself to death, sacrificing all he could, and using all his time and energy in making his church a success.

The great tragedy is that people whose basic need for self-worth has not been met in childhood will, even when they become Christians, enter the church with the idea that God loves them for what they do and not for what they are. The Christian church is full of people who are inwardly driven to work for the Lord for fear of his disapproval, rather than for hope of his approval. This means that they do far more than they should and far more than God expects. To such people I say, 'If you went to sleep on the floor of the church for a year and never did another thing, when you woke up God would love you just as much as he did when you went to sleep!' We don't work to be saved—we work because we are saved. And the difference is crucial.

If you see someone in your church doing far more than they should and almost knocking themselves out in the effort, then I can almost guarantee that if you probe beneath the surface, you will find the rumblings of a need that was never met in childhood—the unmet need of self-worth. Such a person needs to see that Christian service, to be truly effective, must flow out of a genuine love for the Lord rather than a fear of his disapproval.

Every person needs to feel a sense of achievement—that he is successful in at least one major aspect of his life. Every human being is motivated by a search for a sense of achievement and adequacy. This need becomes evident in our lives when we reach the age of three, four, or five years. If our parents failed to minister to this need and did not take the time to show us how to perform certain tasks efficiently, then this basic need, being unmet, will most likely intrude into our adult existence.

Achievement is vital to a growing child and is crucial to his identity as a person. If this need is not met then the child will probably develop into an adult who is overcome by constant fear of failure. I once talked to a young man in whom I could directly trace back his fear of failure to the early developmental years of his life. I was a pastor at the time, and whenever I asked this young man to do anything in the church he came up with the excuse, 'I'm afraid I'll make a mess of it.' Taking him aside one day I said, 'Bill, I don't know very much about you, but let me see if I can sketch the first five years of your life. Your parents were nice, kind people who cared for you, protected you, looked after your physical needs, gave you good clothes and good food. They saw that you were in bed on time every night, had at least two weeks' holiday by the seaside every year, and looked after you with loving care and concern. Whenever there was anything to be done, such as digging the garden, hanging a picture on the wall or painting a fence, they would never ask you to do it. You were just left to get on with your school work, and they never once asked you to help with the routine tasks of the home and showed you how these ought to be done.' When I finished he said, 'You have given a pretty accurate picture of my parents. How did you know?' 'There's nothing magical or mysterious about it,' I replied. 'The way you are acting today is really the result of what your parents failed to do in those early developmental years of your life. When I ask you to do something and you say 'I'm afraid I'll make a mess of it,' you are really saying "no one ever showed me what my capacities are and now I'd rather not try in case I fail."'

'But what's the answer?' said Bill. I know only one answer to help a person in this position. It is helping him to discover and develop his basic gift and to see that God has given everyone in his Body, the church, *at least one basic gift,* or the ability to do at least one thing well. Bill's gift, we discovered, was 'serving' (Romans 12:7 PHILLIPS). God had gifted him with the ability to meet the particular needs of others in the church so that they could be freed for greater service.

Within hours of discovering his gift, Bill had an opportunity to demonstrate it and develop it. An extremely gifted musical couple with a rich musical and singing ministry, had for some months been unable to express their gifts: they could not practise due to the demands of their five children. I had known about their problem for some time, but until my encounter with Bill I had seen no solution. Suddenly it hit me. This was exactly the kind of situation which God had gifted Bill to handle. I telephoned him and put to him the problem. At once the gift in him began to operate. Motivated as he was by God to help others take care of difficulties and problems, thus freeing them for wider service, he said, 'I'll take care of the children one afternoon a week. I'll take them to the swimming baths in the park, and if the weather is bad I'll bring them home.'

The day Bill discovered his basic gift and started developing it, was the day his life took a completely new turn. He is now functioning happily in his church, performing an important ministry of releasing others for more active Christian service.

Spiritual factors

The greatest need of every individual is to have a personal relationship with God. Human beings are spiritual beings, and their personalities are never fully developed until they come to experience an *abiding faith in God*. Just as our physical and psychological needs cry out to be met, so do the needs of our spirits reach out to be fulfilled. When we surrender to Jesus Christ in conversion we discover in him the potential to meet our every spiritual need. But spiritual fulfilment comes not merely in one initial encounter, but through a daily relationship with him in the power of the Holy Spirit.

A person cannot be said to be fully whole until the needs

of his spirit are continuously being met. People may have a well-adjusted physical and psychological existence, but until they know God through his Son Jesus Christ they live out their lives on a dull two-dimensional level. It is only when a person relates to God through his spirit that he has the potential of living life as God intended it to be lived.

As some of the problems which occur in the lives of Christian believers have spiritual causes, it follows that a non-Christian psychiatrist or therapist will be greatly limited in his ability to help a person discover a spiritual solution. The Bible says that 'the natural man receiveth not the things of the Spirit of God: for they are foolishness unto him: neither can he know then, because they are spiritually discerned' (1 Corinthians 2:14). This is why we who are truly Christ's disciples must be constantly on the alert to help spiritually ailing brothers and sisters: for if we are not able to help them, then most certainly no one else can!

What are some of the basic needs of the human spirit, which if not satisfied leave a person spiritually deprived and full of problems? *The first need is to communicate with God daily through the reading of his word and by personal prayer.* Just as a new-born baby cries out for milk, so does a Christian's spirit hunger for contact with God through his word and prayer. The Scripture says, 'As newborn babes, desire the sincere milk of the word, that ye may grow thereby' (1 Peter 2:2). The prophet Jeremiah said, 'Thy word was unto me the joy and rejoicing of mine heart' (Jeremiah 15:16). If a Christian fails to fence off a certain part of each day and use it to develop his personal relationship with God, then he will soon begin to manifest the symptoms of spiritual deprivation.

A second need of the human spirit is to experience freedom from guilt and sin. Although at conversion every past sin is forgiven by God, this condition of inner cleanliness has to be maintained in order for there to be proper spiritual adjustment. This means that a Christian must keep short accounts with God. All sin and failure must be dealt with as soon as it arises. We have God's promise that 'if we confess our sins, he is faithful and just to forgive us our sins, and to cleanse us from all unrighteousness' (1 John 1:9). If a person fails to do this, then it will not be long before he develops a spiritual deadness and insensitivity that will show itself in some of the symptoms already described.

A third need of the human spirit is the desire for a changed life. The Bible says that 'if any man be in Christ, he is a new creature: old things are passed away; behold, all things are become new' (2 Corinthians 5:17). Once we come to Christ through conversion, it is God's desire that we daily become more and more like his Son, Jesus Christ. 'For from the very beginning God decided that...[we] should become like his Son' (Romans 8:29 TLB). This means that a Christian has to watch carefully that he does not get involved in things that contradict this purpose. He has to be careful about the places he visits, the companions he keeps, the things he says and the things he does. As the human spirit focuses on Jesus Christ it seeks more and more to become like him. If this need is not met by a changed life-style, one that is in harmony with the Lord Jesus Christ, then the deprivation the spirit feels will lead to spiritual problems.

A fourth need of the spirit is the longing to share Christ with others. If the life of God is encouraged in a human spirit, then that life will seek to share itself with others. This is part of a growing process which goes on in a properly adjusted Christian, which Martin Luther called 'The divine exchange'. The more we share Christ, the more Christ can share himself with us. Whenever we share our faith with someone else, then it begins to mean more to us. Expression deepens impression. Such is the design of the human spirit that it develops only in proportion to the amount we give away. If we don't give away and share the life of God within us, then the spirit will soon sense this deprivation and will register itself in the form of a problem.

A fifth need of the regenerated human spirit is to experience a deep, loving relationship with other Christians. When someone becomes a Christian he discovers that along with the person of Christ whom he has invited into his life, comes the rest of Christ's family as well! God in his infinite wisdom has designed it this way, for he knows that in order for us to enrich our relationship with him, we need to enrich our relationship with the other members of his family, the church. God, being invisible, gives us the opportunity to validate our love in the lives of those whom we can see. The more we love each other, the more we find ourselves loving God. The Scripture puts this truth thus: 'If a man say, I love God, and hateth his brother, he is a liar; for he that loveth not his brother whom he hath seen, how can he love God whom he hath not seen?' (1 John 4:20). This is why it is important that we heed the advice of the writer to the Hebrews when he says, 'Not forsaking the assembling of ourselves together, as the manner of some is; but exhorting one another' (Hebrews 10:25). The more we fellowship with each other and love each other, the greater will become the focus of love which we direct towards God. If we do not take the time to cultivate this love of the brethren, then our love towards God will suffer. We will end up with a certain amount of spiritual malnutrition, because our needs are not being met.

While many regard human behaviour as inexplicable and unpredictable, we know from what we have been discussing that there are good reasons why people behave the way they do. They can be motivated by physical, psychological and spiritual factors, and an understanding of the influence of these various factors is essential before we can begin to unlock the doors of human problems.

All behaviour is an attempt to meet certain needs, and the motivation to meet these needs is tremendously powerful and strong. The crying infant communicates his need for physical comfort and food. The rebellious teenager is not just trying to make everyone miserable; he gets some satisfaction from his behaviour. The young housewife who develops psychological symptoms, such as depression, anxiety attacks or insomnia, is not doing it simply to create problems for herself. These problems serve a useful function in dulling the pain of feeling worthless and inadequate. Although the symptoms may not be consciously fabricated nor deliberately intended, they nevertheless are extremely effective in preventing the worst possible hurt—the conscious admission that the sufferer is insignificant, insecure and inadequate.

If you wish to understand human behaviour, you must ask yourself, 'What need is this person trying to fulfil by his or her actions?' If you can answer that question, and answer it properly, then you are on your way to an understanding of the problem. Keep in mind as a general rule that physical problems need physical solutions, psychological problems need psychological solutions, and spiritual problems need spiritual solutions. This is an oversimplification of the issue, as there are times when a physical problem may have a partly psychological or spiritual cause. But I believe it to be a good handle for those who are beginners in the field of counselling.

A person's unpredictable behaviour serves a useful purpose. People don't set out to be unhappy and disturbed. It's their way of coping with their problems. At every turn, over the years, they have made choices and adopted attitudes that best protected identity adjustment. They take one path because it appears less harmful and threatening than another. It is sometimes difficult to understand why people develop psychological symptoms to cover up for a loss of worth, but when we fully begin to understand the causes, it becomes clear that this adjustment is the most effective and the one with which they can cope. This is the task of the helper then—to help people overcome what caused the behaviour. What was caused can be changed. What was learned can be unlearned. What was initiated can be altered.

4

DEVELOPING BASIC SKILLS

Every profession has its own set of techniques and skills. Medical doctors, for example, adhere closely to specific routines they learned while in training. Mathematicians, astronomers and other scientifically trained groups follow carefully defined principles and procedures in their work. Professional counsellors, too, have developed certain techniques and principles which enable them to effectively help people who have personal problems. And the exciting thing is this—many of the basic helping principles used by professional counsellors and therapists can, with a little effort and practice, become operative in your own life, any time you choose.

Although there are between a hundred and two hundred techniques and skills which a professional counsellor has to learn, the most basic of these can be narrowed down to less than a dozen. Any Christian concerned to increase his or her helping skills will find that learning and practising these basic skills and relying on the Holy Spirit's help to make him or her fully effective in another person's life, can open up a new and rewarding personal ministry.

So make up your mind not only to grasp these basic principles but to practise them until they become part and parcel of your personality. Who knows—perhaps once you have absorbed these principles, God will take you on to a deeper level of this important work.

What then are the basic skills a person needs to learn in order to become an effective people-helper? In this chapter I have narrowed them down to ten. Go over each one carefully. Make up your mind not only to comprehend them but to practise them until they become an integral part of your personality.

1. Be a good listener

There's an old saying, 'Enemies talk—friends listen.' And this is basically true. One of the most useful ways you can communicate care and concern for a person who is in trouble is to listen intently, and attentively, to what he or she has to say.

Dr Paul Tournier, the famous Swiss medical doctor and Christian counsellor, says: 'It is impossible to over-emphasise the immense need human beings have to be listened to...in most conversations, although there is a good deal of talk, there is not *real* listening; such conversations are no more than a dialogue of the deaf.' One teenager said, after talking to a counsellor in our Christian Counselling Centre, 'She's the first person who ever listened to what I had to say.' This was because the counsellor had been trained in the art of listening.

In some circles, evangelicals are strongly criticized for their habit of giving answers before they have properly understood the question. It's called 'the evangelical disease'. If you've caught it, get rid of it. If you haven't got it, make sure you don't catch it.

It's not easy to be a good listener. Most people, when confronted by a friend who is in trouble, want to talk or offer advice. But how can you do that until you have truly listened? We all like to give advice, but sometimes being listened to is what a person needs most. Someone said,

'This is why God gave us two ears, but only one mouth; because he wanted us to do twice as much listening as talking.'

But good listening takes practice; it's actually a discipline. It doesn't come easily or naturally. Listening means more than just hearing what a person says. A counsellor I know expressed the difference like this: 'hearing captures the words a person speaks; listening captures the meaning and the feeling that lies beneath those words.' Listening is the mental step by which we become more aware of the other person than we are of ourselves.

The best definition of listening I ever came across is that given by Norman H. Wright, who said, 'Listening is not thinking about what you are going to say when the other person has stopped talking.' If we try to figure out what we are going to say when the other person has finished speaking, then we are in danger of automatically tuning them out, and we may miss a vital phrase or statement. The Bible says in Proverbs 15:23 that 'Everyone enjoys giving good advice', but later on in the same chapter it says that 'a good man thinks before he speaks' (TLB).

It's amazing how we can tune out people and situations. A friend told me recently that he was driving down his local high street, seeing and yet not seeing, when he suddenly realized that the car in front of him had stopped. His adrenal glands turned almost inside out as he hit the brakes. But it was too late; his tuning out cost him the loss of his no-claims bonus.

The next time you see someone with a problem, say to yourself, 'I'm really going to tune in to this person's need.' Focus on what they are saying and what they are not saying. Forget about what you are going to say when they have finished, and concentrate on listening for those feelings that lie underneath the words. Remember, listening doesn't come naturally; it has to be developed.

Demanding as it may be, it is our Christian responsibility: 'Let every man be quick to hear, a *ready listener*, slow to speak, slow to take offence and get angry' (James 1:19, Amplified New Testament).

2. Evaluate a person's level of need

One important way of increasing your ability to help a person in trouble is by learning to recognize their *level of need*. Why is this important? Because it determines the urgency with which assistance must be given, and helps to clarify the manner in which you ought to proceed.

Professor Paul Welter, a Christian counsellor in the USA, has done all counsellors a service by categorizing human problems into five clearly defined areas: (1) problem, (2) predicament, (3) crisis, (4) panic, (5) shock.

A *problem* he defines in the strict dictionary sense of the word—a question or issue which has a solution. A *predicament* is a question or issue about which there is no easy, or satisfactory, solution. A *crisis* is a very large predicament, usually short-term, but requiring immediate and urgent action. A *panic* is a state of fear or apprehension in which a person becomes disoriented and irrational. *Shock* is a dazed or numbed condition in which a person's mind may lapse for minutes or even hours.

Now let's take an imaginary counselling trip through these levels of need in order that we can identify them more clearly.

One night Sarah, an unmarried Christian girl you met at a youth camp some years ago, telephones you out of the blue to say that she has come to live in your area, and can you help her to find a good medical doctor. It's a problem requiring a specific answer, to which you find it easy to respond. You suggest several names to her, and by so doing you have solved her *problem*.

A few weeks later she telephones you again, and

suggests it might be a good idea to get together for a cup of coffee. When you meet she confides in you that she is suffering from a high degree of anxiety. The doctor has given her a prescription for Valium, but as she is opposed to the taking of any kind of drug she doesn't know what to do. She has now moved to the *predicament* level.

Giving advice, which worked at her *problem* level, is not so easy now. In any case, advice is not going to be helpful until she feels that you are concerned not merely about her problem, but about her as a person. You remind yourself also, at this stage, to keep the whole matter in the strictest confidence. So you listen attentively, and let her know that you care.

Two weeks later your paths cross once again, this time while you are walking down the local high street. Sarah immediately bursts into tears as you ask her how she is, and she confides in you that she is three months pregnant. Her family do not yet know, and what is more, she is afraid to tell them. She is obviously agitated, apprehensive, and overwrought. Sarah is in a state of *crisis*. The most helpful thing you can do in a crisis is to give your undivided attention, so you take her for a simple meal and help her think through the issues.

Early next morning she telephones you to say that she has told her family the news, but their extremely negative reaction has brought her to the point of *panic*. 'I'm holding a full bottle of sleeping pills in my hand,' she says, 'and I'm going to take them all as soon as I put this phone down'—which she does without giving you an opportunity to say anything. You, as a helper, also feel a little panic. But, breathing deeply, you manage to regain control. You drive hurriedly over to Sarah's home to find that although she has not taken the sleeping tablets, she is obviously in a state of *shock*. Her dazed expression tells you that she is not able to act for herself, so you act for her. Picking up the phone you call for some medical attention and stay with her until the help she needs arrives.

Most of the issues we meet from day to day are in the area of problems and predicaments. Learn to cope with these to the best of your ability, and you will then be better prepared to move on to handle the complications that arise in the higher levels.

3. Accept people as they are

One hurdle, which some Christians find difficult to over-come when seeking to help a person with a problem, is the ability to accept people *as they are*. Sometimes when listening to a person share a problem, they find themselves thinking, 'How in the world did he get into a mess like this?' or 'Why doesn't she just snap out of this depressed mood?'

Unless we take steps to eliminate these condemning attitudes, we will not be able to offer our best. Judgemental thoughts, whether we realize it or not, will affect the tone of our voice or the expression on our face. This will in turn seriously impede our ability to be an accepting person.

Fiona, caught in the grip of an unhealthy sexual habit, decided to talk it over with Jane, an older and more experienced Christian friend. As Fiona began to share her problem, she was met by Jane's shocked amazement. 'Oh no, Fiona, *not you!*' Needless to say, from that moment Jane's ability to help Fiona was seriously restricted. She made the mistake of relating to her not as she was, *but as she wanted her to be*.

Does this mean that we must adopt a non-judgemental attitude to sin when we know it to be present in a person's life? Certainly not. But we must learn to hate the sin without hating the sinner. The most important thing in counselling (as we have said) is relationship. As we listen to a person's problem in an accepting and non-judgemental atmosphere, a relationship develops. As the relationship grows, the issue of sin can be dealt with later—and dealt with more effectively, because the person has found in you a measure of compassion and understanding.

But how do we keep from developing judgemental attitudes? This used to be my big hang-up when I first started counselling. Whenever people shared their problems with me, I found myself thinking, *'If he had stayed away from the wrong crowd, this would never have happened...'; 'He should have known better...'; 'A little common sense could have prevented this...'; 'A good lecture should sort her out...'.* One day I shared my difficulties with an older minister and counsellor, who said, 'That used to be my problem, too—and this is how I overcame it.' Reaching into a desk drawer he took out a stone and a rusty nail. 'I keep these here,' he said, 'for a special reason. The stone to remind me of the text, "Let him who is without sin...be the first to throw a stone," and the nail to remind me what a Friend did for me a long, long time ago on a hill called Calvary.' Since then, whenever I counsel anyone who has gone astray, I say to myself, 'There, but for the grace of God, go I.' I reason thus—if I had received the same kind of upbringing, developed under the same kind of values, lived through the same experiences, as the person before me, then I might have have ended up doing exactly the same things.

Our moral standards may prevent us from approving a person's actions or life-style, but we should love him *as he is*. Then, accepting him as he is, our love flows out to help him to become the person he should be.

4. Empathize with hurt feelings

John Powell, in his book *'Why Am I Afraid to Tell You Who I Am?'*, claims that there can be no real communication between human beings until they relate to each other on the level of feeling. In other words, you can know a person's thoughts, ideas, values, judgements and opinions, but until you know how the person *feels* you are still standing on the doorstep of his life, instead of sitting down in the living room. This identification with his feelings is called *empathy*.

Although originating with the Greeks, the word has crept into our language from the beautifully expressive German word *Einfühlung*. It means 'to insinuate yourself into a person's feelings so that you feel what they feel, and look out at life through their eyes'. The way to a man's heart (and for that matter, a woman's also) is not through the stomach, but through the feelings.

When training counsellors in the art of empathizing with a person's feelings, we describe for them a typical counselling problem. Then we ask them to identify the hurt feelings in the situation. This gives them practice in putting a handle to hurt emotions.

Ever tried to grasp escaping gas, or take a handful of fog? This is what it's like to try to understand a person's damaged emotions if you can't put a label on the hurt feelings.

Les, sitting in the counselling room, was desperately trying to express how he felt when his counsellor said, 'Sounds like you felt rejected, Les,' 'Yes, that's *exactly* it,' said Les. From that moment onwards in the counselling session Les felt more confidence in his counsellor. He realized that even though his counsellor might not be able to solve his problem, at least he understood. When we take the trouble to identify people's feelings and say, 'I imagine that made you feel pretty frustrated' or 'I can see how you felt a little fear in that situation', it enables the person with the problem to feel a little more understood. When you help a person understand his feelings, he understands himself better and he understands you better.

Practise trying to empathize with people's hurt feelings. Put a label on them in your mind when next you are confronted with someone who is emotionally hurt. Ask yourself, 'Is this frustration, disappointment, anger, resentment, anxiety, rejection,' and so on. Draw out those feelings and reflect them back to the person. It will never fail to help your friend feel understood.

5. Be careful what you say, and how you say it

When we have listened attentively to a person's problem, accepted him as he is, locked into his inner feelings, and evaluated his level of need, the time comes when we are expected to make some verbal comment on the situation. At this stage, what exactly do we say?

Well, let's look first at what we should not say. Don't say, 'Well, I suppose all of us, at some time or other, go through a similar experience to what you describe.' This kind of response, because it doesn't take the person seriously and is no more than a meaningless cliché, effectively shuts off further communication.

Then again, don't slap someone on the back and say heartily, 'Cheer up. What you need to do is to put the truth of Romans 8:28 into operation in your life, and begin to praise the Lord for your problems.' It is certainly true that praising the Lord brings a great deliverance, but before you hammer home that truth there are other issues that have to be cleared up.

Actually, this is why there are so many in the church whose problems remain unresolved. They hear someone say, 'Christians shouldn't have problems. If we praised the Lord they would go away.' They reason to themselves, 'I'm not supposed to have problems, so I'll bury them and drive them underground.' But problems that are buried don't *stay* buried; they continue to work at unconscious levels. Jesus always allowed people the privilege of expressing their negative emotions. He never once reprimanded anyone for expressing his or her hurt feelings.

Another remark to avoid is, 'Well, I hope things go

better for you from now on. I'm sure they will.' This again shows no real interest in the person.

Well, what *do* we say, and how do we respond properly to a person's problem or predicament? Here are three simple guidelines.

(i) *Reflect a genuine interest and concern.* The book of Proverbs (which, by the way, contains God's thoughts on counselling) says, 'Oil and perfume rejoice the heart, so does the sweetness of a friend's counsel that comes from the heart' (Proverbs 27:9 TLB). Show real concern for the *person,* not merely the problem. You can say something like this, 'I'm sorry to see how this problem has hurt *you.* Looks like you've been having a difficult time.' Then pause. The pause will help prevent you from rushing in with a slick piece of advice. It can be used also to convey, in non-verbal language, your own personal grief and concern.

(ii) *Reflect back to the person a summary of the problem as you see it.* One way to be sure that you have heard correctly, and also to give assurance to the counsellee that you have understood what he has said, is to repeat back to him a summary of his problem. You might say, 'Let me reflect back to you what I am hearing you say so that there can be no possibility of my misunderstanding the problem.' In doing this you are making clear to the counsellee that you really want to understand his problem. It enables you to check whether or not you have grasped the situation correctly, and eliminates the possibility of miscommunication.

(iii) *Don't give advice—help the person think the issues through.* You may have a clear solution to the person's problem, but remember that if you solve a person's problem for him he will probably return when something else goes wrong *expecting you to solve that problem, too.*

Toss in a few questions, such as 'How do you think this problem can be resolved?' 'Does the Bible have anything to say on this subject?' 'What do you think this verse of Scripture means in relation to your problem?' Pointed questions such as these can challenge a person's thinking and set him in the direction he should go. A good counsellor tries to work himself out of a job. He helps a person think things through by presenting the issues in such a way that the person ultimately answers his own questions. I know it's not as easy as it sounds. But you can make a start next time you meet a friend who is in difficulty.

6. Distinguish between causes and symptoms

Unless you understand the difference between causes and symptoms you cannot expect to bring more than limited help to a person. The prophet Isaiah recognized the need of looking beneath the surface in order to find the cause of a problem when he wrote, 'he shall not judge after the sight of his eyes, neither reprove after the hearing of his ears' (Isaiah 11:3). Behaviour such as losing one's temper, flying off the handle, throwing objects across the room, or similar attitudes or actions, are symptoms and not causes. And the causes, like the roots of a tree, are often hidden.

When you seek to help someone with any kind of problem, don't make the mistake of focusing on the symptoms—behaviour rather than causes. For example a young girl I know went to the youth leader in her church to share with him a problem that had developed in her life—that of nail-biting. The youth leader, failing to understand the difference between a symptom and a cause, began to focus on the symptom. He said, 'Cut your nails short and keep them that way. If that doesn't stop you, then paint your nails with something distasteful so that you won't be able to stand the taste.' The youth leader continued to give free advice, concentrating on the behaviour (the symptom) rather than the cause.

Fortunately, the young girl later shared her problem with someone who understood the difference between symptoms and causes. He encouraged the girl to express herself and share from the depth of her heart just what it was that was bothering her. As she shared her problems, it became evident that she was suffering from a bout of pre-examination nerves. Now that the cause was discovered, the counsellor began to focus on her anxiety and shared with her an insight that helped her to resolve her problem. He said, 'God has a plan for your life which takes into consideration every detail of your existence. Even if you failed your examination it would not interfere with God's spiritual purposes for your existence. And if you do fail then you can have another opportunity to try again. So let's pray about this and surrender the whole thing into the Lord's hands.' As he prayed, the girl said, 'I just felt the Lord reach down into the depth of my heart, dissolve my anxiety and give me such a wonderful peace.' The nail-biting stopped. And what's more—she passed her examination!

7. Keeping confidences

Can you keep a confidence when someone shares with you a personal problem? If you can't then you ought not to be involved in the ministry of helping people with their problems. The Scripture says, 'He who goes about as a talebearer reveals secrets, but he who is trustworthy in spirit keeps a thing hidden' (Proverbs 11:13). Another verse from the same book says, 'He who goes about as a tale bearer reveals secrets; therefore associate not with him who talks too freely (Proverbs 20:19, Amplified Bible). Can you see what the Scripture is saying here? It is warning us that if we know someone who is a gossip and can't keep someone's personal problems a secret, then we shouldn't associate too much with that person.

What is told you in confidence should be kept in confidence. This means that no information should be shared without that person's permission. Many people intend to be confidential, but often they let information leak out through carelessness. Just because a person is a relative or a friend, does not mean that we should share with them the confidences of other people. All personal information must be guarded as a sacred trust.

Some time ago I was called in to resolve a problem in a church: one of the members of a team of counsellors had shared with a deacon of the church a confidence that had been given him. The deacon, thinking he was doing the right thing, shared it with his family round the dinner table, asking them to pray about the person's problem. One of the children present at the table immediately raised the matter in the Sunday School during the afternoon, and soon almost everyone in the church knew about the problem. Needless to say, the person who had originally shared the problem, ostensibly in confidence, was devastated and deeply hurt.

In some countries a doctor, minister, or lawyer is protected by law from being forced to reveal information that has been given to him in confidence. Surely a Christian counsellor has no less responsibility.

8. A wise use of questions

A mistake many people make when attempting to help a person with a problem is to ask too many questions. If you ply a person with too many questions he will conclude (i) that counselling is simply the answering of questions and (ii) that once the questions have been asked and answered then he will be given the solution to his problem. This puts an undue pressure on a counsellor and should be watched right from the start.

Dr Gary Collins has devised some guidelines on this matter which I, personally, have found extremely helpful. He says,

(i) *Ask open-ended questions*—those questions that can't be answered with a single word, such as 'yes' or 'no'. For example, if you say to someone, 'Do you feel your parents are part of your problem?' they might reply 'yes'—which reveals little information. A better way is to ask, 'What are some of the ways in which your parents have influenced you?' Questions that can be answered with a single word should be avoided. They turn an interview into a question-and-answer period.

(ii) *Avoid either/or questions.* These are questions that present two alternatives. For example: 'Do you want to get married or remain single?' The person may respond with his or her preference and then discussion stops.

(iii) *Ask indirect questions.* Direct questions are straight enquiries; indirect questions enquire without seeming to do so. 'How does it feel to have your marriage break up?' is too direct. Put it this way: 'I wonder how it feels to have one's marriage break up.' The latter helps a person to feel that he is not being quizzed.

(iv) *Avoid a series of questions.* Too many questions, one after the other, is extremely threatening. Avoid this at all costs.

(v) *Ask 'Why?' sparingly.* 'Why?' is a useful word to elicit information, but it carries a connotation that is threatening and foreboding. In school, at work and in the home, whenever anything goes wrong someone asks, 'Why did you do that?' The word 'why' therefore has a negative ring. If it has to be used, fill the word with warmth and understanding by your tone of voice.

9. Watch your body language

Dr A. Mehrabian, in his book *Silent Messages,* discusses the importance of non-verbal behaviour in human relationships. His research into this subject indicates that any message between two people consists of three parts: (1) the actual words, (2) the tone of voice in which those words are uttered, and (3) non-verbal behaviour—for example: facial expression, body posture and general appearance.

In the past couple of decades a new behavioural science of communication called 'kinetics' has blossomed. In popular terminology this means 'body language'. Some researchers believe that body language influences the opinions and behaviour of people as much as words do.

Dr Mehrabian claims that the actual words we use to communicate any given message make up only 7% of the communication process. The tone of voice we use to convey the message makes up another 38%. But the biggest part of the whole is made up by non-verbal language: the look in our eyes, the expression on our face, or the way we position ourselves bodily. This makes up a startling 55%. So it's not just what we say, but the way we say it, that counts!

If we are to communicate effectively with those we are trying to help, we must realize the power of non-verbal language. Take the eyes, for instance. Think of how we use our eyes to communicate our feelings: we wink, stare, glance, and shed tears. We widen them in surprise, or narrow them in suspicion. 'We can,' says one Christian counsellor, 'humanize or dehumanize a person with a single look.' If we really care about people we should look at them when we minister to them. If we continually look away when talking or listening to them, the message they get from our non-verbal language is that we are not interested, or that we are embarrassed, or indeed that we do not agree with them and are unwilling to consider their viewpoint.

Gestures are another important component of body language. We use them to communicate our feelings, sometimes unconsciously. We wave goodbye, threaten with a clenched fist, point out directions, cross our arms in defiance or boredom, or tap our feet in nervous rhythm. When attempting to help a person with a problem, don't sit with crossed arms and crossed legs. This suggests defensiveness. Lean towards the person when you talk. This is a sign of interest and involvement.

When you tell a person that you are interested in his problem but deny it by your body language, you create what psychiatrists call a 'double bind'. This is a contradiction between words and actions. It instils confusion and anxiety into the person you are trying to help. Realizing that our body language needs to be consistent with our words is a major step in being an effective people-helper. Christ created our bodies, so he understands perfectly well how they operate. Our bodies are the temple of the Holy Spirit, so in setting out to help people let's aim to do it with everything we have—spirit, soul and body. Then we will become, as Paul said, 'living letters of truth to be read and known to all men' (see 2 Corinthians 3:2).

10. Don't be drawn in out of your depth

As much as you would like to help *every* person that comes your way—it isn't possible. Now and again you are going to meet people with problems beyond your capacity to assist. And if you don't recognize this, and you strive to help everyone who has a problem, then it won't be long before you will be needing help yourself.

Dr Gary Collins says, 'One of the most significant ways in which we can help people is to refer them to someone more equipped and better able to help them than ourselves.' To do this is not an admission of failure; it is a mature recognition that none of us can help *everybody*.

Diane and Carol were having lunch together. 'Diane,'

said Carol, 'I get so frustrated with my husband, Peter. He is so irritable. Believe me, submitting to him is not easy.' (Diane thinks, 'I'd like to ask her what's wrong, but I'll just let her know that I hear. Maybe I can help by being a good listener.') Carol continued, 'He just won't face up to the problems we are having with our son David. Peter refuses to even talk about it.' (Diane senses that this is no time to give advice, so she just empathizes with Carol's feelings and reflects back that she feels her hurt.) 'I imagine it feels pretty frustrating, huh?'

'When the pastor preaches about submission,' said Carol, 'I feel I want to scream. He ought to change places with me for a while; then he might preach differently. How can I overcome this problem?' (Diane realizes she is getting out of her depth. So she gently and lovingly supports her friend, letting her know that she feels her hurt, understands her reaction, and will stand with her in prayer throughout her difficulties.)

But more is needed: she needs to refer Carol to someone able to solve her problem regarding submission. So she says, 'It must be hard for you, Carol. I can sense your hurt. Perhaps you need to see how Scripture teaches you to handle situations like this. Let me call Bill Matthews at the church. He's had some experience in counselling. He's very good, kind, considerate, and deeply understanding. He'll help you to see how the Bible can solve your problem, and he'll do it without making you feel as if you should never have sought his advice. Meanwhile, I'll make it a matter of special prayer and we'll keep in touch to see how things are going.'

Whenever you feel that the problem you are facing in your friend's life is outside the limits of your own insight or experience, refer him to someone better able to help. He will not feel rejected when you hand him over to someone else, providing you assure him of your continued support in prayer and an occasional meeting together.

5

THE GREAT COVER-UP

One of the most fascinating things about the human body is its ability, when damaged, to defend itself against further injury and hurt. When we sprain an ankle, for instance, the body relays a message to the mind informing it that until the ankle has had time to recover, the weight of the body must largely be supported by the other leg. We cut our finger, and what happens? Within a few days, providing the body's defence system is functioning as it should, a scab appears. The scab is nature's defence, protecting the wound from further injury and the entrance of disease-carrying germs. When the wound has healed, the scab just drops away—mission accomplished.

A similar defence system can be seen at work when we enter the mysterious world of the human personality. The mind, for example, has its own anaesthetic. When through a serious accident or some other contingency we suffer more pain than we can endure, the body comes to our aid by gently pulling down a blind on consciousness—we faint. Those who find life in the world of reality unbearable and intolerable are offered an escape route into the world of fantasy. 'Insanity,' says one psychiatrist, 'is nature's way of helping troubled individuals find a less painful world in which they can exist and one with which they are more able to cope.'

Many people carry within them a great deal of fear and anxiety. Sometimes nature helps them to cope with this problem by shaping the general fear into a particular fear known as a *phobia*. A phobia is a morbid dread of a specific object. Rather than allow a person to be weighed down by an anxiety for which there appears to be no definite cause, the personality seeks to relieve this general anxiety by constricting and restricting it to particular moments. Some people have a fear of closed-in places. This is called *claustrophobia*. Some people have a fear of open places. This is called *agoraphobia*. Others are unable to face the possible perils of heights. This is called *acrophobia*. All these phobias (and there are many others) are designed to relieve the constant tremors of anxiety a person carries within himself. They accomplish this by focusing his fears on to specific objects or circumstances by which he is confronted only at odd times and on special occasions.

The same thing happens in the case of what we call a 'guilt complex'. This has to do not with real guilt, but with imagined guilt. It is the haunting sense of moral evil, or sinfulness, which sometimes afflicts people who have been brought up by severe or harsh parents. This complex carries with it a need to be punished. Although some people find this difficult to understand, a person who is deeply afflicted by a sense of guilt will unknowingly and unconsciously seek to bring about self-punishment.

As with anxiety, the human personality has devised a way to relieve the suffering caused by a guilt complex. Just as anxiety constricts itself into a phobia, so the guilt complex gathers itself up into what psychologists call a *scruple*. The word is derived from the Latin word *scrupulum,* meaning a small pebble. We have all experienced the intermittent stab of pain that comes as the result of a small stone or pebble getting inside one of our shoes when out walking. So a scrupulous person, walking through life, feels from time to time the intermittent pain of his imagined guilt. A scruple usually focuses on some supposed sin or moral violation. As a phobia gathers up a general anxiety so that it does not weigh down the personality every single moment of the day, so a scruple gathers up the generalized sense of guilt, constricting and concretizing it.

All defences, whether physical or psychological, fulfil only a temporary purpose. They are nature's devices to help us cope with the problems of an imperfect world. In an environment where there were no accidents, sickness or disease, physical defences would be unnecessary and unknown. Similarly, in a world where there was no moral or emotional disturbance, the defence mechanisms of the personality would also be unnecessary and unknown. In this chapter my purpose is to introduce you to the major psychological defence mechanisms that operate in the lives of those who have been psychologically hurt. You can know them, understand them, and know how to help people avoid them by dealing with the root issues.

Before examining in detail the various defence mechanisms that operate within the human personality, let's consider why it is that defences arise in the first place. The question might be asked, 'In using defence mechanisms, what are people defending *against*?'

Basically, it is a defence against the loss of self-worth. This is not the only reason, of course, but it is the primary one. Each one of us has certain basic needs in our personality which, from the earliest days of our existence on this earth, cry out to be met. We have a need, for example, to belong to a close-knit family unit which develops a growing and loving relationship. We have a need also to be able to contribute to life and to do at least one task effectively and well. But the greatest need, one that is uppermost and dominant in all our personalities, is the need to feel a worthwhile human being. When these needs are not met, defence mechanisms arise within our personalities to help us cope with the sense of loss and to help dull the pain that follows such deprivation. Although any unmet need brings considerable distress to the personality there is no doubt, in my mind at least, that the most hurtful negative feeling a person can experience on this earth is the feeling of personal worthlessness. It is the most damaging, the most painful, and the most corrosive of all the negative feelings that can arise within the human heart. This statement might come as a surprise to many, so at this point allow me to bring a few simple psychological facts into focus.

From the moment we arrive in this world each one of us begins a search for self-worth and self-identity. 'Every baby born into the universe,' says John Powell in his book *Fully Human Fully Alive*, 'is a living question mark.' The first question asked is about self: 'Who am I?' The answers that a child receives in the early years of his life will determine whether he will grow up with a negative or a positive self-concept. If the child's parents are deficient in meeting his basic need for love, and loves him only conditionally, the answers the child will give to the question 'Who am I?' will greatly hinder his healthy psychological development. He will say to himself, 'I am loved only when I am good,' or, 'I am loved only for what I can do...what I look like...or when I am useful to others.' If these are his conclusions, then that child is on his way to a diminished psychological existence on this earth. He will suffer the most damaging blow the personality can sustain—the loss of self-worth.

The personality, however, (as we have seen) is extremely adaptive at coping with such problems. To dampen the feelings of loss it will provide a whole variety of defence mechanisms. The subconscious suggestion is given that if genuine love is not available then one must settle for the next best thing—*attention*. The child will then begin to manifest extremely unacceptable behaviour on the proverbial basis that attack is the best form of defence. This results in the child feeling the lesser pain of rejection for what he is. He finds it much easier to live with the knowledge that he is being rejected for his unacceptable behaviour than with the knowledge that the rejection is due to his own worthlessness.

As no parents or foster parents, however kind and considerate they may be, can *fully* meet a child's basic psychological needs, this means we all arrive in adult life with some or many of these defence mechanisms operating in our personalities. To the extent that we allow Jesus Christ to fully meet our needs, to that extent our defences come down and we become, as one writer puts it, 'fully human and fully alive.'

When I once lectured on this theme to a class of students who were training to be counsellors, one of them said, 'If most people live out their lives behind these defence mechanisms, then isn't it our task as counsellors to point out these defences and encourage them, with Christ's help, to step out from behind them and trust God to meet all their basic needs?' I pointed out to the questioner that the solution is not quite as simple as that. We should never try to get rid of people's defences, but to concentrate on the problems that cause these defences to be erected. When the cause is dealt with, then the defences come down automatically. Quite simply, the personality has no further need for them.

I wish I had understood this a little more clearly when, in the early days of my counselling ministry, I talked to Veronica, a young woman suffering from deep depression. After discussing with her for some time her symptoms, I rather naïvely remarked, 'Has anyone ever told you why people get depressed?' 'No,' she said, 'I don't think I have ever had that explained to me.' 'Well,' I went on, 'let me explain it to you. Depression is really a device of the personality which comes to your aid to damp down the feelings of worthlessness that you have deep down inside your being. Not all depression comes about for this reason, of course, but mostly this is the cause.' 'But,' she protested, 'nothing can possibly be worse than the feeling of blackness and despair that comes over me when I am depressed.' 'Ah,' I said, sensing the cut and thrust of an interesting argument, 'you may think that there is nothing worse than the awful feeling of blackness and despair that comes over you when you are depressed— but believe me, that is a hundred times easier to cope with then the feeling that you are not a person of worth.' To this Veronica gave no reply, but I could see from the expression on her face that she was thinking deeply. Suddenly she began to tremble and shake violently. For a few moments I was gripped by panic, not knowing what to do; but fortunately, whatever was causing this problem lasted no more than two or three minutes.

Veronica started to sob quietly, and as I waited for her to recover her composure I suddenly realized what had happened. My remarks, albeit innocently intended, had removed all her defences. I had stupidly reached out and demolished the protective device that her personality had provided her with. Now here she was, like a hare caught in the blinding headlights of a car at night, trembling, blinking, not knowing which way to turn or run. It took four or five hours of gentle counselling before Veronica could leave the room and go out and face life again. Believe me, from that day to this I have been careful not to remove people's defences by indiscreet statements and inappropriate remarks. Instead I have focused on ministering to the root cause of the problem, leaving the defences to fall of their own accord.

Defences perform an important function. They help prevent an individual from being shattered by a situation, and allow him time to gather strength to deal with it.

Unfortunately, they also prevent the individual from coming to grips with the situation. The more mature a person is, the less defensive he needs to be. Christ had no defences. He did not need them. There was nothing in his life for which he had to defend himself, and his perfect openness and honesty is a model for those of us who follow him.

The knowledge we gain from examining the defence mechanisims of the personality must not be used to browbeat people, or force them to maturity. Keeping this in mind, let's examine some of the major mechanisms by name.

Repression and suppression

Psychology teaches us that below the conscious mind are the two levels of the subconscious and the unconscious. The subconscious is that part of our mind which, lying immediately below the conscious, contains memories, attitudes, and experiences which are largely forgotten by the conscious mind, but which at certain times and under certain circumstances can be recalled and retrieved. The unconscious mind is that deeper area where attitudes, events, experiences, and memories are buried so deeply that apart from the application of certain psychological techniques, they cannot be recalled by the conscious mind. Someone has described the conscious, subconscious, and unconscious minds as being like a bungalow with a large cellar. The living accommodation is the conscious, the cellar is the subconscious and the unconscious. When we cannot face or live with an attitude we find in ourselves, we sometimes bury it in the subconscious and hope that it will no longer trouble us. If the problem is extremely serious the personality will bury it deep in the unconscious, where it will be firmly forgotten by the conscious mind. The problem is this—unacceptable events, memories, and attitudes are never buried dead, but alive. What is more, they remain alive.

When unacceptable things are pushed down into the subconscious mind in an effort to be forgotten, and stay at that level, this is known as 'suppression'. The memory, event, or attitude is forgotten by the conscious mind, but on occasion it emerges into the conscious—only to be firmly suppressed one more time. This kind of thing can go on indefinitely. It's rather like sitting on a powerful jack-in-the box that keeps on popping up and having to be pushed down. 'Repression' is a similar principle except that the unacceptable memory, event, or attitude is pushed so deeply into the lower levels of the mind that it lodges in the unconscious, and is usually beyond the ability of the conscious mind to recall.

Rationalization

This has been described as 'the most common form of ego defence'. It is finding a reason for our actions and attitudes which is not the real one. For example, when I was a pastor a woman complained to me about her husband who was a heavy drinker, and asked me if I would speak to him about it. When I confronted him with the reality of his behaviour, he skilfully employed the defence of rationalization by informing me that the only reason he drank beer was because it had malt in it! Try as I might, I was not able to get behind his defence. The real reason why he drank was because he liked it; it released him from his inhibitions and helped to make him feel secure when he was with others.

There is always something which a person cannot admit to himself—something he would like to do which appears wrong, or something that would make him feel better if he could believe it. Rationalization is the bridge that turns wishes into facts. A little boy being bullied by an older and stronger boy in the school playground afterwards remarks to a friend, 'I didn't hit him because it was beneath my dignity.'

Rationalization is the use of one's intelligence to deny the truth. It makes us dishonest with ourselves—and unless we can be honest with ourselves we will certainly not be honest with others.

Projection

This is a defence mechanism by which a person attributes to someone else his own thoughts and feelings. 'I can't stand pompous people,' confessed a young Christian girl in a counselling training class. Later on, when she was working in one of the small-group sessions where there was a great deal of openness and honesty, the whole group reflected to her that she came across to them as a very pompous person. Unconsciously, she had been projecting on to others the thing she disliked in herself.

Projection is the device we use to rid ourselves of our limitations by attributing them to someone else. Adam and Eve did this. Adam explained his sin to God in these words: 'The woman whom thou gavest to be with me, she gave me of the tree, and I did eat' (Genesis 3:12). Eve also made good use of this device: 'And the woman said, The serpent beguiled me, and I did eat' (Genesis 3:13).

Betty, a personable but plain teenager, came to me for counselling, complaining that a number of married men in her church were trying to flirt with her. After a few sessions of counselling it became obvious to me that this was not the case, and that she was projecting her own desires on to the men concerned. Eventually she came to see this for herself.

It is a very common human tendency to dislike most in others what we cannot accept in ourselves. And the reason why we can't see these things in ourselves is simply because they are repressed. Whenever we overreact to anything, dislike someone or something intensely, we should examine the situation to see whether or not we are using the device of projection.

Introjection

This is the ego defence by which a person attempts unconsciously to make himself like another person, or to attribute to himself the characteristics and qualities of that other person. By means of identification the first person behaves as though he was not himself but the other person, deriving satisfaction from sharing his successes or failures.

Jean, a young mother and housewife, came for counselling regarding what she described as 'her addiction to the afternoon soap operas'. Every day after lunch she would put the baby to bed, then settle down to watch the TV soap operas. Slowly she had become addicted to the television presentations and would allow no one to enter her home during those early afternoon hours, keeping the doors locked and the curtains drawn. It took me a long time to show her that because of her weak and insecure ego, she was identifying with the TV characters as an escape route from the grim world of reality into a world of fantasy. It was providing her with a degree of romance and interest which was not actually present in her rather dull and unromantic marriage. As she came to see that her basic needs could not be met by such behaviour, and learned how to bring Christ's love and power into her personality, the desire for identification with heroes and heroines dropped away. She found in the reality of Christ's love a satisfaction that no amount of TV identification could ever give her.

Introjection is prominent in teenagers when they go through the phase of what we call 'hero worship'. Some grow out of it, but many don't. As they become adults they identify with possessions or money and take pride in the fact that someone praises their home, or admires them for belonging to a well-known fraternity, or for having attended a famous school. By means of this ego device we are able to behave as though we are not ourselves but some other person, deriving a sense of satisfaction from sharing either their success or failure.

Compensation

The great psychologist, Alfred Adler, first became interested in compensation as a defence mechanism when he noticed how one kidney did the work of two when the other failed to function. Working from this principle in nature he observed how the human personality also attempts to compensate in some way or other for a deficiency, real or imagined. Those, for example, who have feelings of inferiority or insecurity may act in a superior, self-assured or sophisticated manner. Or a person with demoralizing doubts in the subconscious mind will cultivate the position of someone who is extremely dogmatic and sure of everything. People who are over-tender, to the point of being extremely sentimental, sometimes assume this attitude in compensation for harsh and cruel tendencies which have been repressed into the subconscious mind.

Compensation has been described as 'leaning over backwards to avoid tipping forward'. Exaggerated behaviour in anyone usually means the very opposite of what it implies. John, a buyer for one of London's department stores, shared with me a problem which illustrates how this ego device works. He told me that he was unable to sleep at night because of a great concern for his eighty-year-old mother with whom he was living. The old lady was certainly ailing, but far from being ill, and he was unable to understand why he should suddenly feel such an exaggerated concern. In the third session of the counselling programme I set up, I talked to him about the possibility of a subconscious desire to be free of the responsibility of caring for his aged mother. At first he rejected this suggestion, but later came to accept it. When he did accept the fact that he was carrying a subconscious wish to be free of responsibility for his mother, and saw that his exaggerated concern was a compensation for this, the insight he gained was all that was necessary to bring the whole situation into perspective. Facing the repressed desires he dealt with them, accepted them and was troubled no longer with sleepless nights.

It would be wrong, of course, to suspect every concern and good inclination to be a psychological cover-up or a defence mechanism at work. Only exaggerated behaviour ought to be suspected of being this defence mechanism.

Displacement

This takes place when we express indirectly an impulse which our conscience or training forbids us from express-ing directly. For example, a child may develop as he grows up a strong resentment and hostility towards his parents. The child's conscience will monitor these feelings, and tell him that it is quite wrong and improper to have such feelings towards his parents. The child then represses these feelings but, in order to get rid of the bitterness and hostility which he had to repress, directs them towards smashing property—or something equally irrational.

A common form of displacement is the device of disguising an unpleasant event or attitude to which we cannot admit (and thus repress or suppress) by consciously laying stress upon some issue or subject which is not so embarrassing to the ego. We worry and become concerned over a small matter, which is really quite trivial, to conceal some greater fear or difficulty which we would rather not face. Sometimes a husband and wife will do this in a marriage relationship. Deep down they despise each other, but rather than get to the source of their mutual difficulty, they will argue and quarrel with great vehemence about trivialities.

Displacement occurs also when a person becomes jealous of another and will not admit to his jealousy.

Usually the jealous person alights on some trivial deficiency in the other person and makes, as we say, 'a mountain out of a molehill.' It may take the form of criticism of the envied person's voice, hairstyle, vocabulary, or any other personal feature. Displacement goes on in our personalities far more than we realize. But as we have said, it's no good trying to get rid of the defence without first making sure that what caused it in the first place has been remedied.

Sublimation

This is the device by which repressed impulses (particularly the sexual) are directed towards new aims and activities. Let me pull this a little more into focus by telling you about Mark. Mark, a fine-looking teenage mechanic, came to me at the Counselling Centre and began the interview by asking if I would pray with him that God would take away his sexual drive and desires. When I enquired as to why he would want me to join him in this kind of prayer, he said, 'It's ruining my spiritual life. I masturbate several times a day. I find myself with lustful thoughts towards several girls in the church, and I feel so dirty that I just can't go on.' 'Getting rid of your sexual drive,' I said, 'is not the answer. It's like cutting off your nose to spite your face.' I went on to explain that the sex drive is the thing that gives fire and sparkle to the personality. Without it we would be dull and lifeless individuals.

What Mark needed was to take this strong sexual drive and channel it into more acceptable and rewarding activities. It needed, in other words, to be sublimated—directed towards new goals and new ends. The sex drive is a creative one, and it seemed to me that harnessing this drive toward creative ends was the answer. I suggested to him ways in which he could begin to use this creative drive towards more purposeful and spiritual ends. He began to spend more time in planning a creative programme of

Bible study and Bible meditation, as well as working out ways in which he could be of use and service to Jesus Christ. As he focused on this and became involved in more creativity in his spiritual life he found that his sexual urges, although still strong, were well and truly under control. This kind of sublimation is a wholesome, constructive type of adjustment.

Intellectualization

This takes place when a person avoids the emotionally disturbing aspects of something by attempting to treat it in a detached, objective manner. This is a favourite defence among educated people and those who may wish to consider themselves educated. It is a device of the personality whereby feelings and ideas are kept separate and never allowed to meet.

In the famous story of Christ's meeting with the woman of Samaria, as described in John 4, we see this ego device at work. The woman was perfectly prepared to discuss where God should be worshipped, whether at Jerusalem or on Mount Gerizim. But Christ moved the issue from the realm of her intellect to the realm of her emotions by a gentle pressure on her conscience, commanding, 'Go, call thy husband.' Jesus quietly got behind her defences by showing her that God wants to establish his throne not merely in a city or on a mountain, but in the human heart.

Non-Christians use this defence to a great degree when confronted by the claims of Jesus Christ. One preacher tells how as a minister in a small village he was confronted by the local wag, who said he had been having difficulties with the 'kenosis' theory—the theory of Christ laying aside his divine attributes and taking upon himself the form of a human being. The minister suspected that this was an intellectual device to keep him away from the real issue—personal sin and the disturbed feelings that accompany it. So he gently brought the conversation round to the fact that the man's real problem was not so much with the kenosis theory as with the Decalogue. He had broken God's commandments and was a sinner. When the man was confronted by this, he saw that his intellectualization was a defence to keep attention away from the disturbed feelings he knew he would have when confronted by the need to repent and be converted.

Through intellectualization a deeply-disturbed person may sometimes deceive even a trained counsellor (as well as himself) into believing that he has no problem.

There are several other forms of defence which the personality uses to defend against further damage to a sense of personal worthlessness, but the ones I have already dealt with are the most common. It is important to remember that a defence mechanism operates in order to keep a person's psychological being intact. A person who is unable to live comfortably with reality exercises repression or suppression. I say again, don't take it upon yourself to chase people out from behind their defences. Concentrate rather on helping a person see that his or her deep need for significance, self-worth and security can be fully and totally met in Jesus Christ. When he or she sees this, really sees it, then the personality will realize that it no longer has need of defences and will lower them of its own accord.

Now that you are aware of how these defence mechanisms work, examine yourself to see how authentic is your own personality. The people-helper who cannot face himself and his own methods of evasion will have little understanding of these devices when used by others.

6

A STRATEGY
FOR HELPING PEOPLE
THROUGH THEIR PROBLEMS

When teaching in the Crusade for World Revival's Institute in Christian Counselling I am often asked by trainees if, when attempting to help someone in difficulty, I have in mind a simple plan or strategy. My usual reply to that question is to say that there are several models that I follow, adapting each one to the particular situation or circumstance. When pressed to share the model that I have found most useful I refer them to the strategy first developed by Dr Robert Ellis, and known to experienced counsellors as R.E.T.—Rational Emotive Therapy.

Before I bring Ellis' model of counselling a little more fully into focus, it ought to be noted that there are in fact about 200 different theories on the subject of how best to help people through their problems. However, these theories can, broadly speaking, be narrowed down to three basic areas—behaviour, feelings and thoughts.

Some counsellors believe that the sole task in helping people through their problems is to focus on changing their behaviour. 'Right behaviour,' they say, 'is obediently doing what God wants, and is the single key ingredient of spiritual growth.' Other counsellors believe that the primary task in counselling is to help a person ventilate and express disturbed feelings. 'Once a person expresses, understands and accepts his deepest emotional experiences,' they claim, 'he will feel altogether different and his symptoms will vanish.' Another group of counsellors insist that the real issue in counselling lies in changing a person's thoughts and that to be effective one must focus on this cognitive domain.

I believe that although there is a place in Christian counselling for helping people develop new patterns of behaviour and for empathizing with hurt and troubled feelings, any form of counselling which stops short of changing a person's thoughts is, in the long term, ineffective and unproductive. I believe this to be the view of Scripture also, as pinpointed in Romans 12:1-2 and expanded in other passages of both Old and New Testaments.

Let's return now to the subject of Rational Emotive Therapy, as presented by Dr Robert Ellis, and ask ourselves, 'What is it, and how can it be used in the field of Christian people-helping?' Dr Ellis presents his model in five stages:

1. The Precipitating Event (What caused the problem)
2. The Belief System (How a person perceives the event)
3. Consequent Emotional Reaction (What emotions are aroused by the perception)
4. Counteracting Questions (Disrupting the distorted views)
5. Answering the Previous Questions (Re-interpreting the issues)

Before examining Ellis' strategy for counselling in detail, I should say that while this model can be used for most problems, it does not cover every difficulty that arises within the human heart. Sometimes, for example, a person experiences anxiety and concern which arise from within, rather than being triggered by a precipitating event. In such cases this model needs to be adapted, and a thorough grasp of the strategy will leave you in no doubt as to the right approach when faced with such a difficulty.

1. The precipitating event

Ellis claims that the first thing to be considered in building a strategy for counselling is the precipitating, or activating, event. In other words—what caused the problem? It could be one of many things, such as a broken engagement, losing a job, the death of a loved one, failing an examination, and so on. A counsellor's first task is to explore the precipitating event in order to comprehend the full nature of the surface problem. In order to do this effectively we must remind ourselves of several of the principles we discussed in the chapter 'Discovering Basic Skills'.

Firstly, *we must listen.* Remember our definition of 'listening'? 'Listening is not thinking about what you are going to say when the other person has stopped talking.' If when listening to a person we focus on what we are going to say when he has stopped talking, we might miss a vital piece of information. This, in turn, could prevent us from comprehending the full nature of the person's problem.

Secondly, we must *ask appropriate questions until all relevant facts are understood.* The operative word here is 'appropriate'. Don't probe for additional facts in order to satisfy your own curiosity. Your purpose is not that of obtaining information for yourself.

Thirdly, *evaluate the level of the person's need.* Ask yourself: 'Is this a problem, a predicament, a crisis, a panic, or shock?' A correct conclusion in this area will help you determine the urgency with which assistance must be given.

Fourthly, we must *tune in to a person's hurt feelings.* This means tunnelling your way into the person's heart so that you begin to feel as he or she feels about the specific problem or difficulty. This kind of empathy has been described by someone as 'your pain in my heart'.

Fifthly, *reflect back to the person what he is saying—in*

your own words. Say such things as, 'Let me see if I understand your problem correctly. You are feeling angry because everyone in the youth group was invited to the party, but for some reason you were not.' Or, 'It seems to me that you are saying that although you are engaged, and have set a date for the wedding, you are not sure whether this is the person God wants you to marry.' After a reflection has been made the person should be given an opportunity to respond—even if this consists of telling you that you have missed the point completely!

2. The belief system

This is the area where a counsellor examines the counsellee's evaluation system in an attempt to discover how the counsellee perceives his world, and how he interprets it. One of the most debated issues in psychology concerns the role of thinking in the determination of behaviour. Ellis believes that the starting point of emotional problems is not the event, but the person's evaluation, or perception, of that event.

Don Dulaney, an American psychologist, has gathered evidence to show that how a person interprets his world, what he believes to be in it, and what value he attaches to the various elements in it, greatly influence and control his feelings and behaviour. He has systematized his thinking into what he calls his Theory of Propositional Control, a theory which Ellis builds on in R.E.T.

Let me try to interpret for you, as best I can, the view of Ellis and Dulaney in relation to the Theory of Propositional Control. In the early years of our lives (say between birth and five years old) we gain our basic assumptions about life. Our first achievement is to build a vocabulary of words such as chair, table, door, and so on. Later we learn to put those words into sentences, and the kind of sentences we then use forms our basic assumptions about life.

Take the following example. A child, having learned the words 'chair' and 'table', proceeds to push the chair against the table, only to find that the chair stops. He becomes frustrated at this and it is here that parental guidance plays an important part. A discerning parent, recognizing that the child is having his first lesson on the principle of cause and effect, will help the child to see that although the chair is blocked by the table, it is possible to get around the problem simply by moving the chair in a different direction. The child, if guided correctly when confronted with such a problem, will soon begin to say to himself, 'When I push the chair against the table it stops, but if I push it to one side, then I can get around the table and solve the problem.' Dulaney claims that because we are self-conscious beings, we can talk to ourselves in sentences and the sentences we learn to put together in the early developmental years of our lives play a strongly determinative part in our later development.

A parent may be unaware of how a child's self-image is formed and developed, and fail to intervene, guide, control and instruct a child in the art of overcoming frustration. If he or she neglects to show the child that when problems occur there is usually a way round them, then the child might well conclude that the world is full of problems that are too big and complicated for him to handle. Furthermore, if a parent fails to show a child unconditional love, and demonstrates love only when the child behaves in a way that is acceptable, then the child will begin to put together sentences such as this: 'The world is full of problems that are too big for me to handle. My parents don't love me, or love me just some of the time. I can't be a very good person. What's the use of trying? I'll just give up.' In a fascinating review of experiments, Ellis and Dulaney show that when an external event catches our attention, we respond to it firstly by talking to ourselves about it. We may not always notice the words we say, but, nevertheless, we respond to all situations in propositional form, that is, we clothe our impressions in words. Those sentences will reflect, to a great degree, the basic assumptions about life which we develop in the formative years (between birth and five years), and it is these basic assumptions which constitute our belief system and play a great part in the determination of our feelings and behaviour.

It is simply amazing how, even as adults, we talk to ourselves in sentences that reflect the inner self-rejection, hatred, inbred fear and insecurity we felt when we were children. We may not notice the sentences we use but we do, nevertheless, respond in verbal form to most of life's difficulties and situations.

Jim, a top salesman for a large international firm, woke up one Monday morning to discover it was raining heavily outside. He immediately became depressed, and when his wife asked him why, he mumbled words that sounded like, 'because it's raining outside'. This wasn't quite accurate, because rain in itself has no power to make anyone depressed; but a strong negative mental evaluation of the storm does. Jim's wife, a counsellor who had been trained in examining a person's belief system, encouraged Jim to explore the sentences he was saying to himself at that moment. This is what transpired. 'This morning I promised to play golf with a client from whom it might be possible to obtain a large order for my firm. He is due to leave town this afternoon and it is most unlikely that I will get the order sitting with him in an office. I know he will be disappointed that he cannot play his usual round of golf. This order, if I secured it, would help me financially to make some renovations to the house. Now it looks as if I can say 'goodbye' to it.'

His wife then pointed out to him that it was not the rain that was making him depressed, but his evaluation of it.

As she shared with him the fact that even though he might not secure the order for which he was striving, there was so much they could both be thankful for, he saw that he had allowed himself to become dependent on circumstances rather than God. As Jim saw the truth his wife was sharing with him, he knelt down and prayed this prayer: 'Lord, I am so thankful that it rained today, for if it hadn't I might still be trying to live this day independently of you. Thank you for showing me that *you* are my supply—not circumstances or people. If I secure this order today then I will praise you for it. And if I don't secure it, I will still praise you. Thank you, Father, for what you have taught me through this situation.' Later that morning Jim got his order—one that was bigger than he had ever expected.

A counsellor should, therefore, learn to pay a good deal of attention to the fact that when confronted by a problem, a person will talk to himself about it. The counsellor's task is to gently probe this area in an attempt to discover the person's basic assumptions about life. In what terms does he see his problem? Does he view it as an obstacle to be overcome, or does he see it as a setback that will become, in God's hand, a springboard? At this stage in counselling, I usually ask such questions as these: 'How do you feel deep down inside about this problem?' or, 'If you were in God's place, would you have prevented it from happening?' The answers that are made let me know something about the person's belief system—how they see life and how they perceive and evaluate their world.

The next stage to which counselling then proceeds, is this:

3. Consequent emotional reaction

The way a person sees an event, says Ellis, is largely responsible for the negative emotions that are aroused. For example, if a loved one (Person A) dies, the person who is left behind (Person B) is deeply grieved. What causes the grief? You might say, 'Why, the death of Person A made Person B unhappy.' But suppose Person B despised Person A—what then? The death of Person A produces in Person B a feeling of relief that Person A is not going to be around any more. In other words, the event does not control the feeling, but the evaluation of the event does.

Ellis calls this the ABC Theory of Emotion. A (what happens to you) does not control C (how you feel); B (what you say to yourself about A) is directly responsible for C (how you feel).

Apparently, then, it is not so much what happens to us as how we perceive it that is important. When someone is criticized he often feels a good deal of displeasure and anger, which is then vented on the one who has expressed the criticism. Many people think that the criticism has produced the anger, but this is not so. Prior to the reaction of anger something happened in the person's thoughts and it was this that produced the anger. We often hear the statement, 'You make me so angry.' Think about it for a moment. How can anyone *make* another person angry? Do they achieve it by injecting some substance into the blood-stream? No. The person becomes angry when he responds wrongly in his thoughts. It is this, not the other person, that makes him angry.

Let's return for a moment to the Theory of Propositional Control. What might be going on in the mind of the person who has been severely criticized? Might it not be this? 'It is humiliating to be criticised and it makes me feel utterly worthless. This is how I felt when I was a child, when my parents treated me as if I were an object and not a person. It isn't fair. I shouldn't be made to feel like this, so I will defend myself and hit back at the person who has wronged me.' As we have seen, negative reactions such as anger, depression, and hostility are really defence mechanisms against a further loss of self-worth. When our basic assumptions about life are challenged we are inwardly motivated to protect ourselves from the painful feelings which a loss of self-worth brings. Such things as alcoholism, compulsive spending, over-eating, excuse-making, and a host of other behaviours are an attempt by the personality to anaesthetize or compensate for the emotional pain of feeling worthless.

It must be said again that it is not so much what happens to us as how we perceive it that matters. And how we perceive it will depend to a great extent on how we learned to put sentences together in the early developmental years of our lives. If those sentences are negative responses, drawn from the pool of our basic assumptions about life, and contain thoughts or ideas that strike at the roots of our self-worth, then it will not be long before they trigger off emotions that produce unhappiness, distress and psychological pain.

It should be noted that the three most negative emotions that arise within a person when he or she carries wrong basic assumptions or incorrect perceptions are these— *resentment, guilt* and *anxiety*. Watch out for these three problem emotions. You will find them coming up again and again in your counselling encounters.

Having explored the theory that it is not the event that triggers off negative emotions within us, but our perception of the event, how do we deal with the negative emotions when they arise? Ellis claims that there is little point in trying to change a person's emotions. It is more productive, he feels, to concentrate on changing the thoughts that were responsible for producing these emotions. This brings us to his next step.

4. Counteracting questions

Here we set about challenging a person's basic assumptions, thoughts and beliefs. But how does this work in practical terms? When a person says 'I am angry' (consequent emotion) which proves, on exploration, to have arisen from someone having criticized them strongly, then look for the in-between reason—the basic assumption or belief. It becomes necessary to challenge those basic beliefs by questions such as these:

> Why do you become so distressed when you are criticized?
>
> Is there something in your background that is triggering off memories, making you react in this way?
>
> From where do you get your understanding of your self-worth —from what people say about you or from what God says about you?
>
> What is the base of your security—the opinion of others, your family, or what?

The use of carefully placed questions can help to open up a person's mind to see how utterly futile are his wrong basic assumptions about life. Keep in mind that, up to this point, no solutions are offered. The purpose here is simply to prise open the person's mind by challenging his basic assumptions about life.

Just before sitting down to write this chapter I was involved in one of the Crusade for World Revival's Family Life Seminars. In one of the intervals between the sessions a young man grabbed me and said, 'Please give me a few minutes of your time. I have just been jilted by my girl-friend. We were due to be married in four weeks' time. I'm feeling very depressed. What shall I do?' I had about three minutes to say something meaningful, and so I followed the procedure I am outlining here. Since the precipitating event was undoubtedly that of the broken engagement and the consequent emotion (in this case anxiety) arose from the young man's perceptions of the event, I put to him the following three questions: 'Do you believe that Romans 8:28 applies in your particular situation?'; 'Do you believe God had you in mind when he inspired Paul to write those words?'; 'How are you going to apply James 1:2-3 (PHILLIPS) to your problem?'.

I sensed that these piercing questions went deep into the young man's heart, but asked lovingly and with compassion I believed them to be the best I could do under the circumstances. When the seminar was over he told me that he hadn't heard a single word that had been said in any of the lectures. 'I have been focusing,' he said, 'on Romans 8:28-29 and James 1:2-3.' 'And what have those scriptures done for you?' I asked. This was his reply: 'They were the pegs I needed to hang my troubles on.'

A counsellor should build and prepare sentences that go right to the heart of people's problems. Remember, however, what I said a few paragraphs ago; at this stage you are not seeking to offer solutions, but simply to draw the counsellee's attention to the fact that his emotional reaction is due not to the precipitating event but to his perception of it. In other words—to his faulty thinking.

Dr Robert Ellis has identified what he calls Ten Irrational Ideas (views) that lead to destructive feelings and even to mental illness. Ellis concludes that health and balance are restored when these irrational viewpoints are replaced by rational ones. The Ten Irrational Ideas, slightly simplified, are listed below.

Ten Irrational Ideas

I am responsible for getting, or remaining, hurt if I keep irrationally thinking that...
   (i) I must be loved and accepted by those who are most important to me, and live up to their expectations.
  (ii) I must be perfectly competent and successful in achieving before I can be happy with myself.
 (iii) It is easier to avoid certain difficulties and responsibilities rather than face them; if I ignore them they might go away.
 (iv) Certain people are bad and deserve blame or punishment for their sins

   (v) I must be prepared for the worst by constantly dwelling on what may be bad, dangerous, or feared.

  (vi) I have been shaped by the past, and it is too late to change.

 (vii) It is terrible when things do not go the way I have planned.

(viii) I have no control over my own happiness: what happens to me determines my happiness.

  (ix) I must find the quick and perfect solution to my problem.

   (x) It is easier to keep doing things the way I am doing them without taking on new commitments.

Ellis trains his counsellors to challenge these wrong basic assumptions by such counteracting questions as these:

You say that life is terrible. Apart from what has happened to you, where is your evidence to support that view?

Although I admit that what has happened to you is terrible—does this mean that you are terrible?

Tell me—why should this not have happened to you?

Is there any law which says that you, and you alone, must be exempted from the trials and difficulties which fall upon others?

Because this has happened to you, does it mean that life has come to an end?

Are you going to stay tyrannized by the past, or are you going to break free and start to live life as it should be lived?

It goes without saying that these and similar questions must be presented lovingly, tenderly and compassionately. To present them unfeelingly would make them counter-productive, to say the least. With a little thought you can soon build up a series of questions that go right to the heart of the matter. Work on them week by week until you have a small library of well-shaped counteracting questions. This brings us to the fifth and final stage in our model.

5. Answering the previous questions

This involves answering the questions which were raised

in the previous phase. It ought to be obvious by now that R.E.T. proceeds on the basis that most problems stem from distortions of reality based on faulty and erroneous thinking. This is an approach to counselling which I believe to be in harmony with Scripture. 'As [a man] thinketh in his heart, so is he' (Proverbs 23:7). This last phase of our counselling model (Answering the Previous Questions) will come easily to a Christian counsellor, for working with that authoritative volume, the Bible, we have all the resources we need for correcting wrong basic assumptions, faulty presuppositions and erroneous thinking.

'By correcting erroneous thought patterns,' says Ellis, 'then the emotional responses can be changed. *If you think right you will feel right* (italics mine). He goes on to say that in helping a person come to terms with the fact that what is causing his problems is wrong thinking based on wrong assumptions, the four following guidelines ought to be kept in mind:

  (i) A person must be made aware of what he is thinking.
 (ii) A person must be shown that some of his thoughts are inaccurate and erroneous.
(iii) A person must be taught how to substitute accurate thoughts for inaccurate ones.
 (iv) A person must be given feedback from an outside source to help him evaluate whether he is making the right changes.

It is precisely at this point that Christian counselling demonstrates its superiority over every other form of approach. The best that Ellis (and other non-Christian counsellors) can do is to re-interpret the issues of life within a strictly secular frame of reference. He deals with such things as self-acceptance, developing a positive self-image, and other psychological axioms within a humanistic framework, and thus his efforts are only partly beneficial.

The Christian counsellor, basing his approach on biblical axioms, works to re-interpret the counsellee's life in terms of God's will and purpose. He presents to the counsellee the unimpeachable facts of Scripture and shows him that in all of life's struggles and problems, God allows only what he can use. When the omnipotence and sovereignty of God are even feebly apprehended, it enables a counsellee to place his problems against the bigger and wiser purpose of a loving Creator.

A Christian people-helper must be able to intelligently assert and defend the proposition that God never allows anything to happen to one of his children unless he sees that by allowing it he can make it work for good (Romans 8:28-29). He must also be able to show that every one of our personal needs (significance, security and self-worth) can be fully and adequately met through a personal relationship with Jesus Christ. True significance does *not* depend on whether I own my own house, have a prosperous business and drive a Rolls Royce: it depends on understanding who I am in Christ. If I fail in business; if my wife leaves me; if I live in a small flat or bedsitter; I can still experience the thrilling significance of belonging to the King of kings who has designed me for a unique task in his universe.

Take again the need for security. This need presses inside me to demand that I be unconditionally loved and accepted as I am. In Christ I have access to this kind of love. I am completely acceptable to him regardless of my behaviour. God may not like my unscriptural behaviour, but this makes no difference to his acceptance of me. It is true that all unacceptable behaviour must be dealt with, but even his disciplines are full of love. The eternal God has pledged his power to operate on my behalf so that nothing will happen to me that he doesn't allow. That's security.

And what about self-worth? After close on thirty years working in the area of Christian counselling, I have come to the conclusion that the most devastating feeling one can experience on this earth is the feeling of utter and complete worthlessness. It is this (as we reviewed in the chapter on Defence Mechanisms) which is responsible for so many psychosomatic ailments we see in today's society. When a person's sense of self-worth is injured he will find a way to hide from it, and retreat behind protective symptoms. Sometimes these symptoms produce a good deal of hurt and pain (depression, for example). But this pain, bad though it may be, is far less hurtful than the awful blackness and emptiness a person feels when he is forced to face his feelings of worthlessness. Better to hurt badly for other reasons and maintain a sense of worth, than to be relieved of the suffering the symptoms bring and to feel utterly worthless.

My sense of worthlessness, however, can be banished as I reflect on the fact that God loved me enough to give his Son to die for me. The Scripture records that 'While we were yet *sinners* [Greek: sinning] Christ died for us' (Romans 5:8). If God loved me before I became his child (while I was yet sinning) then how much more will he love me now that I belong to him through the new birth!

The counsellor's task then, in this fifth phase of our model, is to reinterpret the issues of life within God's frame of reference. It involves the use of scriptural insights so that the counsellee can begin to interpret his life from God's point of view. Let's look again at the Ten Irrational Ideas which Ellis lists, and see how we can interpret these ideas within a biblical perspective. I shall list the ideas as before and then add to each one what I consider to be an appropriate biblical point of view. (All quotations are from the RSV.)

I am responsible for getting, or remaining, hurt if I keep irrationally thinking:

    (i) I must be loved and accepted by those who are most important to me and live up to their expectations.

Matthew 5:11; 'Blessed are you when men revile you and persecute you and utter all kinds of evil against you falsely on my account.'

(ii) I must be perfectly competent and successful in achieving before I can be happy with myself.
2 Corinthians 12: 9-10; 'My grace is sufficient for you, for my power is made perfect in weakness.'

(iii) It is easier to avoid certain difficulties and responsibilities rather than face them; if I ignore them, they may go away.
Luke 9:23; 'If any man would come after me, let him deny himself and take up his cross daily and follow me.'

(iv) Certain people are bad and deserve blame or punishment for their sins.
Luke 23:34; 'Father, forgive them, for they know not what they do.'

(v) I must be prepared for the worst by constantly dwelling on what may be bad, dangerous or feared.
1 John 4:18; 'There is no fear in love, but perfect love casts out fear.'

(vi) I have been shaped by the past and it is too late to change.
2 Corinthians 5:17; 'If any one is in Christ, he is a new creation; the old has passed away, behold, the new has come.'

(vii) It is terrible when things do not go the way I have planned.
Mark 14:36; 'Father, all things are possible to thee; remove this cup from me; yet not what I will but what thou wilt.'

(viii) I have no control over my own happiness; what happens to me determines my happiness.
Matthew 6:22-23; 'The eye is the lamp of the body. So, if your eye is sound, your whole body will be full of light; but if your eye is not sound, your whole body will be full of darkness.'

(ix) I must find the quick and perfect solution to my problem.
Philippians 4:5-6; 'Let all men know your forbearance.

Have no anxiety about anything, but in everything by prayer and supplication with thanksgiving let your requests be made known to God.'

(x) It is easier to keep doing things the way I am doing them without taking on new commitments.
1 Corinthians 13:5,7; 'Love does not insist on its own way.... Love bears all things, believes all things, hopes all things, endures all things.'

This, then, is the major area on which a Christian holds focus—the bringing of every thought into subjection to Christ, so that feelings and behaviour flow out from a heart committed to 'seeing life from God's point of view'. This does not mean that you must at times not give your attention to the areas of feelings and behaviour. But in-depth counselling works through these two levels (behaviour and feelings) in order to reach the third —*thoughts*. God has built into us a specific design—what we think about effects the way we feel and how we feel affects the way we act. If when counselling we seek to follow this divine design, then our task will be made easier and our successes greater.

TRACING SURFACE PROBLEMS TO THEIR
ROOT CAUSE

1.	THE PRECIPITATING EVENT	WHAT CAUSED THE EVENT? 1. Listen intently 2. Ask appropriate questions 3. Evaluate the level of need 4. Tune in to hurt feelings 5. Reflect back what is being said
2.	THE BELIEF SYSTEM	HOW DOES THE PERSON PERCEIVE THE EVENT? 1. Discover what sentences the person is saying to himself 2. What are the person's assumptions?
3.	CONSEQUENT EMOTIONAL REACTION	WHAT EMOTIONS ARE DISTURBED? 1. Is there resentment against what has happened? 2. Is there guilt due to the violation of biblical principles? 3. Is there anxiety due to misplaced dependency? 4. Is there a combination of two, or all three?
4.	COUNTER-ACTING QUESTIONS	WHY SHOULD THIS DEMORALIZE YOU? 1. Dispute the basic assumptions
5.	ANSWERING THE PREVIOUS QUESTIONS	WHAT DOES GOD SAY ABOUT THIS SITUATION? 1. God only allows what he can use 2. God alone is able to meet our three basic needs 3. God loves you and has a wonderful plan for your life

7

THE USE OF
SCRIPTURE IN PEOPLE-HELPING

If up to this point you have read through this book systematically, chapter by chapter, one thing should by now be quite clear—*God uses people to help people.* The story of the raising of Lazarus from the dead is an excellent example of this principle.

> 'Then they came to the tomb. It was a cave with a heavy stone rolled across its door. 'Roll the stone aside,' Jesus told them. But Martha, the dead man's sister, said, 'By now the smell will be terrible, for he has been dead four days.' 'But didn't I tell you that you will see a wonderful miracle from God if you believe?' Jesus asked her. So they rolled the stone aside. Then Jesus looked up to heaven and said, 'Father, thank you for hearing me. (You always hear me, of course, but I said it because of all these people standing here, so that they will believe you sent me.)' Then he shouted, 'Lazarus, come out!' And Lazarus came—bound up in the gravecloth, his face muffled in a bandage. Jesus told them, 'Unwrap him and let him go' (John 11:38-44, TLB).

I used to wonder, when I read this passage, why it was that Christ, whose creative word brought Lazarus from the dead, did not use that same power to rid him of his graveclothes. It seems perfectly logical to me that if Christ could raise a man from the dead, then he could by that same power cause his graveclothes to fall away from him.

The fact that Christ turned to those who were standing around and told them, 'Unwrap him and let him go' illustrates a profound spiritual principle. God alone can give a person *life*, but he often uses others to bring about *liberty* in life.

I know many Christians, as I am sure you do, who have the life of God flowing through their being—but they don't have much liberty. They are wrapped round with the graveclothes of damaged emotions, unhealed memories, and repressed hurts. And it is to such people as these that Christ points, when we commit ourselves to be Christian counsellors, and says: 'Unwrap him and let him go.'

In order to help people experience liberty in life, we must learn to use the power available to us in God's word, the Bible. Psychological insights which are in harmony with Scripture are fine, but the greatest power to set men and women *truly* free is the power contained in God's eternal and errorless word. Jesus, when addressing his disciples on this issue, said, 'You are truly my disciples if you live as I tell you to, and you will know the truth, and the truth will set you free' (John 8:31-32 TLB).

As we have seen, there are almost as many approaches to the subject of counselling as there are counsellors. Some see their role as identifying with the person in need—to sit where he sits. Others view their task as simply being a shoulder to cry on; to listen, reflect back what is being said, and help to assimilate hurt and bruised feelings. Almost every counselling approach has something in it that is commendable, but what is most needed today is the ability to speak words that reach the troubled heart and fit deep into the empty socket—words from God.

This does not mean (as we have seen) that we should throw large chunks of the Bible at people without first endeavouring to build a relationship, to empathize with hurt feelings, and to become sensitive to their personal needs.

Of course, before we can begin to use the Bible in

helping people with their problems, we must first be convinced as to its *authority*. It is extremely important that a Christian counsellor believe in the authority of the Scriptures, as any lack of confidence on this issue will reflect itself in the counselling process. Regrettably, the church is at present passing through a phase which some describe as 'the battle for the Bible'. In many sections of the Body of Christ there is a crisis of confidence concerning the Holy Scriptures. Some say the Bible is most certainly without error when focusing on the needs of man and his eternal salvation, but that on other issues its veracity must be questioned. Let me make my own position clear on this matter. I believe the Bible, in its original form, to be divinely inspired and without error in all its parts. I hope you share that view too.

After all, true Christian counselling, or people-helping, is not so much the mastering of certain techniques as being mastered by certain convictions. If you believe the Bible to be the authoritative word of God, you will be able to offer to those you counsel the one thing that non-Christian counsellors (and those Christians who do not have implicit confidence in the Scriptures) are unable to offer—*hope*. Supported by a high view of Scripture, you can approach every problem with the firm assurance that somewhere in the Bible God has a solution for it. With Dr Martyn Lloyd-Jones you can affirm that 'every conceivable view of life and of men is invariably dealt with somewhere or other in the Scriptures'. Biblical principles, because they are authoritative and divinely inspired, are not to be presented in a way that suggests, 'Try this and see if it works.' When presented clearly and applied properly *they never fail to work*.

The power of a wise word of counsel

The right word spoken at the right time can change a life, especially when that word has in it the ring of divine authority. The writer of Proverbs says, 'Death and life are in the power of the tongue' (Proverbs 18:21 RSV). Imagine a tool so powerful that with it you can elevate a person's spiritual vision, deepen his moral convictions and improve the quality of his service for Christ. A properly selected Bible text is that potent! Listen again to the writer of the book of Proverbs as he brings into focus the importance of a true and timely word:

> Everyone enjoys giving good advice, and how wonderful it is to be able to say the right thing at the right time!
> (Proverbs 15:23 TLB)

> Timely advice is as lovely as golden apples in a silver basket.
> (Proverbs 25:11 TLB)

More often than not the timely word is a prepared word, though it appears to be spontaneous. The right Bible passages don't just pop into your mind without some prior reason. They might appear to be spontaneous, but they really arise from a heart that has prepared itself by thoughtful meditation and study. So make up your mind to build a library of carefully selected Scripture passages so that you can use them when attempting to help people with their problems.

In this chapter I want to show you how to apply the right scriptures to people's problems. In order to do that I propose to look at ten of the most popular phrases people use when feeling dejected, dispirited and downcast. Once you grasp the principle of tying in appropriate passages of Scripture to personal problems you can then begin to build your own library of biblical texts on an ongoing basis. In examining the following examples keep in mind what I have said in earlier chapters—that counselling is not just handing out advice (even biblical advice), but a relationship. It is the word becoming flesh—in you.

Example 1: 'I'm feeling all churned up inside.'

A man who shared that statement with me some time ago was on his way out of church following the Sunday morning service. I knew something of his circumstances and to what he was referring. His wife had deserted him a few days previously, leaving him to look after four young children. As he passed through the church door I called him back and, grasping his hand for a few moments, I said quietly, '*God* gives peace.' These three short words, with a special emphasis on the word *God,* conveyed two things: first, a reminder that inner confusion and 'a churning inside' does not come from God; and second, a word of hope—*he does* provide peace. I followed this up with a quotation from Phillippians 4:6-7, which I have memorized for use in such emergencies: 'Be careful for nothing; but in every thing by prayer and supplication with thanksgiving let your requests be made known unto God. And the peace of God, which passeth all understanding, shall keep your hearts and minds through Christ Jesus.'

A few days later I received a telephone call from this man. He said, 'Selwyn, I honestly can't remember much about your sermon on Sunday morning, but those words you spoke to me when you grasped my hand have been a lifeline over these past few days.' I said, 'What words?' Of course I knew exactly what he was referring to, but I wanted to give him an opportunity to recite them back to me, thus deepening their impact on his mind. Without any hesitation he quoted the text exactly as I had given it to him. I found out in the course of our conversation that he had spent hours searching his Bible for that text, and when at last he stumbled upon it he committed it at once to memory. I have no doubt that whenever my friend begins to feel 'all churned up on the inside' he will become his own counsellor and apply the truth of that matchless scripture to his own personal and individual needs.

Example 2: 'I've never known so many things to go wrong. What can be happening to me?'

Ever heard someone use this phrase? What scripture would you consider using to help a person see this particular problem from God's point of view? Let me tell you the one I would share. It is this: *'It is God which worketh in you both to will and to do of his good pleasure'* (Philippians 2:13). In addition to this I would add a few words of my own which, under God and alongside Scripture, can help to bring hope and healing into the situation. I would say something like this: 'God only allows what he can use, just as the only board a carpenter cuts is the one he intends to work with.' Perhaps I would even add to that by saying, 'Have you seen the signs on the side of the road that say "Men at work"?' After waiting for a moment to see that my question was understood, I would say, 'Well, over your life at this moment you have a sign that says "God at work". Don't wrestle, just nestle in the fact that he knows what he is doing, and that through these upsetting situations he is pursuing his purpose to deepen your character and make you more like his Son, Jesus Christ.' I would also read or recite at this stage the Living Bible paraphrase of Psalm 138:8, which I have found to be of special help to people when things seem to be all upside down: 'The Lord will work out his plans for my life—for your lovingkindness, Lord, continues forever'.

Example 3: 'The Christian life has so many rules. I feel hemmed in by them. Isn't there any freedom in being a Christian?'

The verse that at once rises in my mind whenever I hear this type of statement is this: 'This is love for God: to obey his commands. And his commands are not burdensome, for everyone born of God has overcome the world' (John

5:3, New International Version). I usually say, following the reading of this scripture, 'It is not burdensome for a car to run—that is what it is made to do. It is not burdensome for a canary to sing—that is what it was made for. It loves to sing. A commandment to lovers telling them to love would not be burdensome—it would be bliss. God's commandments (or rules) are no more burdensome, if we could see them from his perspective, than wings would be burdensome to a bird. What he commands is what we are made in our inner being to do.'

The person who makes this statement obviously feels a negative reaction to divine direction. One counsellor I know uses the following illustration which, when drawn on a table napkin or piece of paper, is extremely helpful in getting a person to see that God's principles and laws are the fences he erects at the sides of the road to keep us out of the ditch.

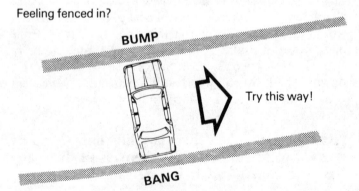

Example 4: 'I'm sure no one has gone through the kind of problem I'm going through at the moment. My situation must be unique.'

Although one can certainly understand a person feeling like this, the Bible says differently. 'Many others have faced exactly the same problems before you. And no temptation is irresistible. You can trust God to keep the temptation from becoming so strong that you can't stand up against it, for he has promised this and will do what he says. He will show you how to escape temptation's power so that you can bear up patiently against it' (1 Corinthians 10:13 TLB).

After reading this passage you might like to say something like this: 'I know how you must be feeling, but let's begin to look at the problem from God's point of view. He claims that no situation is unique because somewhere, sometime, someone else has faced precisely the same problem. This is why God has given us so many biographies in the Bible. They are there to show us that when overtaken by the pressures of life, it is possible to find victory through the power and strength of God and his Son, the Lord Jesus Christ. Let me pray with you and ask God to help you open your life to the strength and grace which is available to you at this moment.'

Example 5: 'I am troubled by wrong thoughts. I try to hold them down, but the energy I am using up in doing this is making me feel a nervous wreck.'

The verse I immediately turn to when faced with this problem is James 1:2-4. I think it is more effective when read from the J. B. Phillips paraphrase: 'When all kinds of trials and temptations crowd into your lives, my brothers, don't resent them as intruders, but welcome them as friends! Realise that they come to test your faith and to produce in you the quality of endurance. But let the process go on until that endurance is fully developed, and you will find that you have become men of mature character with the right sort of independence.' Follow that by saying, 'According to this scripture, every trial and temptation should be treated as a friend. So look upon those wrong thoughts as a friend and thank God for them.' At this point the person will probably counter with, 'What, praise God for wrong thoughts?' You can go on to explain that the procedure of repressing thoughts is both psychologically and spiritually wrong. We must bring everything out into the open, face it and, with God's help, deal with it. When we praise God for wrong thoughts we can actually use the stumbling block as a stepping stone to come nearer to God in prayer. If that action is reinforced by reading an appropriate portion of the Bible, then the evil thought has actually served to deepen our spiritual life and not destroy it. This is known as outmanoeuvring Satan and is one of the most powerful principles of effective Christian living. If the devil is responsible for sending the evil thought then, believe me, when he sees you using it to deepen your spiritual life he will soon give up. Otherwise he will just be doing God's job for him.

Example 6: 'I seem to be getting hurt everywhere I turn. Why is God allowing this to happen to me?'

There are two extremely helpful passages in the New Testament that speak directly to the need of someone with this problem. The first is this: 'And we know that all that happens to us is working for our good if we love God and are fitting into his plans. For from the very beginning God decided that those who came to him—and all along he knew who would—should become like his Son' (Romans 8:28-29 TLB). These two verses of Scripture show us that God has a very significant purpose in allowing hurts and harassments to overtake us. He allows them in order to conform us to the image of his Son. Encourage the person to see the negative things of life as potential positives in God's hands, by which he uses all that happens to make us more like Jesus Christ. A second passage to read is this: 'For he gives us comfort in our trials so that we in turn may be able to give the same sort of strong sympathy to others in theirs' (2 Corinthians 1:4 PHILLIPS). Another reason why God allows some people to go through deep waters is that he wants them to experience a deep sensitivity which can then be used and expressed in the comfort of others. Incidentally, please note that if you want to be a people-helper you can expect God to let you go through experiences where you will get hurt. It is God's major way of teaching you sympathy for the hurts and wounds of others.

Example 7: 'I'm afraid to die. Nothing I seem to say to myself can take away this fear. Can you help me?'

The only way to challenge deep shadows is with the light of God's truth. Old familiar texts leap almost unbidden to the mind at such a time as this. For example, 'Yea, though I walk through the valley of the shadow of death...thou art with me' (Psalm 23:4). Don't fall for the world's carnal approach to this problem that says, 'Support a person by turning their attention towards something else.' If you do this, the person will at some point return to look again into those black depths—and the depths will look even blacker. The Scripture plainly instructs us to 'comfort one another with these words' (1 Thessalonians 4:18). What words? The great truths which are found in the preceding verses. Here is verse 13 as paraphrased by The Living Bible: 'And now, dear brothers, I want you to know what happens to a Christian when he dies, so that when it happens, you will not be full of sorrow, as those are who have no hope.' Read the whole passage quietly, calmly, and deliberately to a person who is distressed at the thought of death.

Another deeply impressive scripture to read is the one found in 1 Corinthians 15:58. Here it is, again as found in The Living Bible: 'So, my dear brothers, since future victory is sure, be strong and steady, always abounding in the Lord's work, for you know that nothing you do for the Lord is ever wasted—as it would be if there were no resurrection.'

Example 8: 'I have been hurt by those who are close to me. It's bad enough being hurt by those who don't love you. How can you cope with being hurt by those who are members of your own family?'

The truth that God is ultimately in control of everything is the insight one should share with this person. I know of no better passage to read than this: 'But as for you, ye thought evil against me; but God meant it unto good, to bring to pass, as it is this day, to save much people alive' (Genesis 50:20). The passage is taken from that beautiful story of Joseph, for whom destiny seemed to turn full circle. Sold by his brothers into slavery and placed in a dungeon in Egypt, he becomes in due course the Prime Minister of the Egyptian nation. Emphasize, too, the beautifully poetic passage where Joseph says: 'You *sold* me...but God *sent* me' (see Genesis 45:4-5).

Another helpful text to share with someone in this frame of mind is Job 42:2. I like to read this from the Revised Standard Version, which states, 'I know that thou canst do all things, and that no purpose of thine can be thwarted.'

Example 9: 'I get so discouraged because despite all my efforts there are still so many areas of weakness in my Christian life.'

2 Corinthians 4:7 is the encouragement this person needs: 'But we have this treasure in jars of clay to show that this all-surpassing power is from God and not from us' (New International Version). Watchman Nee has pointed out the double truth suggested by this verse. We, as human vessels, are very earthly indeed. But the treasure that God has deposited within us by the gift of his Son is glorious beyond compare. *No one can endure the revelation of the one without the other.* Viewing the situation from this perspective can help a discouraged person see his weakness as the motivation for deeper commitment and love for the Lord.

Another helpful verse to read to a person who is discouraged is this: 'And he said unto me, My grace is sufficient for thee.....' The Living Bible puts it, '...he said, "...I am with you; that is all you need. My power shows up best in weak people." Now I am glad to boast about how weak I am; I am glad to be a living demonstration of Christ's power, instead of showing off my own power and abilities"' (2 Corinthians 12:9).

Example 10: 'I can't understand what God is doing. He took away a previous problem, but although I have asked his help in breaking another habit, he doesn't seem to hear me.'

One counsellor I read about likes to use shock treatment whenever he hears anyone presenting their problems in this way. He says, 'Well, if that's the situation, let's get right down on our knees and tell God that according to Luke 11:9, "Ask, and it will be given you", he is just not coming up with the answers he promised.' Then, just before he begins to pray, he turns to the person and says, 'Or do you think the fault might lie within you?' He claims that this short-sharp-shock-type approach has never failed to get the person to see his or her own personal responsibility in the issue.

You might prefer a less revolutionary approach, that of opening your Bible to James 1:13 and reading, 'Let no man say when he is tempted, I am tempted of God: for God cannot be tempted with evil, neither tempteth he any man: but every man is tempted, when he is drawn away of his own lust, and enticed. Then when lust hath conceived, it bringeth forth sin: and sin, when it is finished, bringeth forth death.'

Emphasis must be placed on the fact that every single one of us must accept accountability for our wrong actions. This person, by his own admission, believes that the second habit is something that is happening to him rather than something which *he* is doing repeatedly.

No one, with the Bible before him, can claim that God's standards are beyond his reach, for although he sometimes raises the standards to almost unbelievable heights, he also provides the power by which we can reach up to them.

One of the most effective verses I have ever discovered in the Bible, which relates to this problem and many others, is found in Hebrews 12:15. I have used it on countless occasions and I have found that it carries within it a built-in power which never fails to make a profound spiritual impression on a counsellee, particularly when read from the Phillips paraphrase. Here it is: 'Be careful that none of you fails to respond to the grace which God gives, for if he does there can very easily spring up in him a bitter spirit which is not only bad in itself but can also poison the lives of many others.'

Now that you have had a glimpse of how applying the word of God to people's situations works, make a note of every problem statement you come across and learn to match it with an appropriate and helpful passage from the Scriptures. Memorize as many scriptures as you can and meditate on them until their meaning becomes crystal clear. The more time you give to the preparation of the right scriptures to use in counselling, the more effective will be your endeavours when faced with people who have deep and pressing needs. Some Scripture references for use in various situations are listed in the Appendix at the end of this book.

8

HELPING A PERSON
FACE A CRISIS

How do you react when confronted by someone who is facing a serious crisis? What happens when a friend tells you he or she is about to come apart under the pressure of a major domestic problem? Do you respond to the situation positively and confidently, attempting to steer your friend towards some clear thinking and sound conclusions? Or do you mutter incoherently, stumble for something meaningful to say, and finish up like an Arctic river, frozen at the mouth?

All of us, at some time or another, come face to face with friends, relatives, and acquaintances who are caught up in crisis situations—the loss of a loved one, the discovery of a terminal illness, a financial reverse, the birth of a deformed child, the loss of a job, a broken engagement; any of which are life-shattering events and can leave a person stunned and bewildered. What do we say and how do we help those who are overtaken by such disasters as these?

Before we examine in detail some of the guidelines which can assist us in counselling those who have been overtaken by life's misadventures, let's begin by putting the word 'crisis' under the microscope to see exactly what is contained within the term. A crisis is any event or series of events which threatens a person's well-being and interferes with his ability to cope with daily life. Most people move along the highway of life calmly and efficiently meeting challenges and problems as they arise. Occasionally, however, situations arise which are beyond their ability to cope with, sapping their physical and emotional energy and leaving them disoriented. At such times people are said to be in a crisis.

Let's reflect a little further on what we said in an earlier chapter concerning Paul Welter's categories of people's personal difficulties. You will remember that he divides these difficulties into five clearly defined areas: (1) problem, (2) predicament, (3) crisis, (4) panic, (5) shock. A crisis, says Welter, is a very large predicament; usually short-term, but requiring immediate action. If we accept Welter's definition of a crisis then we will view it as a special sort of predicament. A crisis (again according to Welter) may be expected to last from one to six weeks and the average length seems to be about three.

Most psychologists separate crises into two broad categories: developmental and accidental. Developmental crises are those which occur at predicted times as we make our way through life—the first days at school, coping with adolescence, choosing a vocation, engagement, adjusting to marriage, parenthood, dealing with the insecurities of middle age, and retirement. Accidental crises are much less predictable, and consequently when they hit us they come with greater force. Loss of one's job, an incapacitating accident, illness, an unwanted pregnancy, marital infidelity, divorce, a natural disaster —any of these can produce emotionally hazardous situations and a loss of ability to cope.

How do people actually *feel* when confronted by a crisis? What goes on in their emotional spectra when they find they are unable to adjust to life's major difficulties? Dr D. J. Schwartz, a Christian psychologist, has pinpointed these emotions as follows:

1. A sense of bewilderment: 'I never felt this way before.'
2. A sense of danger: 'I feel so scared—something terrible is going to happen.'
3. A sense of confusion: 'I can't think clearly—my mind doesn't seem to work.'
4. A sense of impasse: 'I am stuck—nothing I do seems to help.'
5. A sense of desperation: 'I've got to do something, but I don't know what.'
6. A sense of apathy: 'Nothing can help me—what's the use of trying?'
7. A sense of helplessness: 'I can't cope by myself—please help me.'
8. A sense of urgency: 'I need help now.'
9. A sense of discomfort: 'I feel so miserable and unhappy.'

Ruminating on life's problems, worrying about what will happen next, questioning why it happened in the first place—these all take up time and a good deal of emotional energy which would normally be directed towards other activities.

But how do we go about helping a person in a crisis? What do we say and what can we do to help a person start moving again in a positive direction? In attempting to help a person in crisis I have discovered that the first prerequisite is a clear plan of action. At this point someone might say, 'I have no psychological training or counselling experience, so any plan of action must be simple enough for me to grasp and apply within the range of my limited experience.' The plan I want to share with you for helping a person in a crisis is something that anyone of average intelligence and sound Christian conviction can effectively use and apply. It requires no great mental effort, no long and wearing hours of assimilation. In fact, it is as simple as ABC.

A—Achieving contact

A person caught in a crisis will feel confused and helpless. To compensate for these feelings, a person will sometimes withdraw into a state of unreality. As you talk together he may alternately look away from you and stare at you as if he is not seeing you. This is because he is caught in what psychologists call a 'sensory overload'. To understand this concept of overload, think of a situation in which you struggled to find an answer to a problem or to recall some fact that kept eluding you. You probably closed your eyes or stared at something without really seeing it in order to keep the visual stimuli from overloading your mental circuit and interfering with your thought processes. A person in a crisis will therefore tend to look at another person without really seeing him, or stare at an object that does not require any mental processing. This is why some people who are depressed and feel down, actually *look down* and gaze at the floor. The first task of a counsellor is to break through this disorientation and make contact with the person. There are several ways in which this can be achieved.

Make contact physically. Whenever I am confronted by a person in a crisis, the first thing I attempt to do is to establish physical contact. If, for example, I find myself standing by someone who reveals to me through their words or actions that he is in a state of crisis, I take him firmly by the arm, steer him towards a nearby seat or chair and say, 'Let's sit down here for a while and talk this matter over.' This simple physical action, if done firmly, deliberately and confidently, helps the person feel that for the moment, at least, someone else is in charge.

Although some counsellors say it is unwise to touch a person when counselling, my own view is different. I fully recognize the dangers that can arise from indiscriminate touching, particularly between opposite sexes. But if done wisely, carefully and tactfully, taking a person by the arm and leading him towards a quiet spot can be extremely reassuring. Scientists tell us that body language is very sophisticated and goes far beyond words. A baby who is not touched, for example, will not develop well. Adults need human contact, too—especially when they are in a crisis.

When I have got the person seated I try to establish eye contact too, as this helps break through the disorientation barrier. In order to do this, of course, one has to sit in front of the person concerned so that visual contact can be made. If a person's sight is impaired I usually sit beside him so that I can make the use of physical touch. These simple physical actions are more than techniques; they are the doors through which you can walk into a person's disoriented and confused world.

One counsellor says: 'Whenever I find myself with someone who is confused or disoriented through a crisis situation, I take care to ensure that all my physical movements speak to him of my own confidence in my ability to cope with this problem. I take the phone off the hook slowly, but deliberately; I let my family know that I don't want to be disturbed (loud enough so that he can overhear my instructions to them); I take hold of my pen or pencil with deliberate firmness so that the person in crisis will feel he is in the presence of someone who knows what he is doing.'

Make contact verbally. When I have succeeded in making contact with a person physically, my next goal is to make contact verbally. More often than not a person in a crisis will increase his rate of speech and allow words to tumble out in a disjointed manner. At this stage a counsellor can say, 'Please slow down because I want to understand what you are saying.' For some people, however, this request is too demanding and requires more self-control than, under the circumstances, they are able to exert. A better way, I have found, is to try to interact verbally with a person in the same way that one would get alongside a person who is walking at high speed—fall into step with him, adjusting your pace to his, and then gradually slow down the pace so that the other person slows down almost without realizing it. I usually do this by asking short, rapid, direct questions, such as, 'What happened then?' 'How did this affect you?' 'When exactly did this take place?', and so on.

After a few minutes of using these short, direct questions, I begin to preface them with statements such as, 'I can see that this has really upset you, and I can certainly understand why you feel the way you do...now tell me what happened next?' The short, direct questions prefaced later by lengthening statements act as a breakwater, slowing down the pounding waves of emotion which flow through the counsellee's being. One must be careful, of course, not to interfere too much with the release of emotion as this in itself can be immensely therapeutic.

I continue asking questions and making statements until I find myself having an equal share in the conversation. You might be asking at this point, 'What concrete purpose does this achieve?' It enables me to tactfully and gently gain control of the conversation so that I can direct it along the lines I want it to go. Up to this point the counsellee has dominated the conversation, pouring out a mixture of explanations, suppositions and fears. If I am to direct him towards more co-ordinated thinking and emotional stability I need to become the leader in the conversation, and not the follower. In counselling circles this is called structuring. It is the process by which a counsellor, through his words, digs a channel into which a counsellee's emotions can flow. The counsellee, overcome by fear and apprehension, will not realize what is happening. After a while, however, he will begin to feel a sense of relief that someone appears to be taking control.

Make contact emotionally. This means making contact with a person's feelings. It involves walking alongside the counsellee rather than leaping ahead to find a possible solution. I feel it necessary at this stage to make clear that in this first stage of counselling, achieving contact, it's not important to search for a solution. This is the mistake many beginners make when attempting to counsel a person with deep problems. They try to start giving answers before they have really understood the problem. People want to know how much you care before they care how much you know. All I am seeking to do at this stage is to interact with the person who is hurting—verbally and emotionally.

The most valuable lesson I have learned in counselling is that it is almost impossible to understand a person's problem until one is able to empathize with their hurt feelings. You can comprehend a person's thoughts and analyse his behaviour, but you will never truly understand him until you know how he *feels*. This means making contact with hurt and injured feelings. How is this done? I usually ask myself when counselling a person in crisis (or indeed, anyone who is obviously hurting over a problem), just what feeling or feelings are hurt. I ask myself: is this frustration, rejection, disappointment, helplessness, fear, or something else? When I am sure that I know what emotion or emotions have been hurt, I reflect back to the person concerned something like this: "I sense that you are feeling deeply rejected right now and I know how hurtful that can be.' Labelling the emotion that has been hurt and reflecting it back to the counsellee enables him to feel understood. In fact, it becomes the bridge over which you cross into his heart and by which he can cross over into yours.

We move now to the second phase.

B—Boiling down the crisis

This involves focusing on the major issues that brought about the crisis. Here again, I am not interested too much in finding a solution, but more in gathering the facts. In seeking to help a person in crisis a counsellor's primary task is to work not with fantasies, suppositions or conjectures, but with *facts*. So I approach this part of counselling with this question in mind: 'What are the major issues that brought about this crisis?'

In order to find these issues one has to resort to probing and analytical questions. One must keep in mind that sometimes the answers a counsellee gives to investigative questions are not true facts, but suppositions and theories. An emotional upheaval can cause a person to exaggerate or misinterpret facts, or even to view conjectures as facts.

In a church I once pastored an unmarried girl came to me in deep distress, claiming that she was pregnant. After seeking to interact with her verbally and emotionally, I then asked her why she thought she was pregnant. Her reply was, 'Because I have missed a period.' I explained to her that thousands of women miss a period, but this in itself is no true indication of pregnancy. I advised her to get her doctor's confirmation on the matter, which she did at once—only to discover that it was not pregnancy that caused her to miss her period, but a temporary case of anaemia. Had I accepted her word on the matter without probing to find the true facts, then I could have involved myself in a good deal of time-wasting. I hasten to add that when this question of her non-pregnancy was established, I counselled her on the wrongs of pre-marital sex and exhorted her to reject this unbiblical lifestyle for one more glorifying to God.

A man came to me in a state of crisis and said that he was about to be declared bankrupt. After a few minutes of working my way into his shattered world and sensitively trying to feel his pain, I felt it was right to boil down the crisis by asking him how much he owed and how many creditors were pressing him. He was reluctant to answer the many questions I put to him, but he shared with me the number of creditors and the amounts involved. Although I have had no legal training I remembered a solicitor telling me that a person cannot be declared bankrupt unless he owes at least one single creditor a minimum of £50. As a small trader his individual debts did not amount to this, so he could not be declared bankrupt. A phone call to a solicitor immediately confirmed this. I then asked the counsellee to arrange to pay off his debts by instalments. The creditors accepted this, so much of the crisis was averted.

In boiling down the crisis, a counsellor's first task is to get the facts. He must ask questions until all relevant factors are understood. Emotion has to be separated from reality, generalizations from specifics. Sometimes a person will omit, exaggerate, forget or simply misinterpret things. A counsellor has to drive his mind like a bulldozer through all the difficulties, separating the facts from the theories and putting them on one side for later attention.

Once the facts have been gathered the next step is to *evaluate the facts* and list them in order of priority. As a result of probing and asking questions a counsellor now has on his notepad a list of facts, some of which may need immediate attention. It is now a simple matter to list these in order of priority. A few years ago a man came to me deeply upset and said that he had come home early from work to discover a note saying that his wife had left him. He pleaded with me to help him try to find his wife by telephoning round to all his relatives and friends to see if she was there. I resisted his appeal and sought first to obtain as many facts as I could. It was fortunate that I did, for I discovered that he had two young children at school who were normally met each day by their mother, but now she had left there would be no one to pick them up and get them home. As I assembled the facts and put them in order of priority, it became obvious that my first task was to help him organize the collecting of his children and arrange for someone to sit with them while we set about the task of tracking down his wife.

Sorting out facts from theories and listing them in order of priority for possible action, is one of the most important aspects of crisis counselling. Some things will have to be done immediately while other things, although important, can be left until later.

The purpose of gathering facts, assembling them, and giving them an order of priority is that then the most pressing issues can be dealt with right away and the crisis dealt with in as workmanlike a manner as possible. For example, if a young child has run away from home it is no good spending time lecturing the parents on how to build unity in their family—steps must be taken to find the child, and to find him as quickly as possible.

Once the urgent practical issues have been dealt with and immediate steps taken to reduce the impact of the crisis, the next step is to help the person learn from the crisis and use it as a stepping stone to greater spiritual depth and understanding. This brings us to the third and final stage of the counselling process.

C—Correlating the issues

I believe my most important task as a Christian counsellor is to enable a counsellee to evaluate what has happened to him from a biblical perspective, and to learn to see life from God's point of view. Over the years I have developed a simple three-point scriptural strategy, which I share with the person at this stage. There is no greater instrument for pulling a confused mind back into clear focus than the word of God. The points are:

God is on the throne. I attempt to show them that no matter how bad the crisis may appear to be, the Almighty is right there in the centre of it. I usually support this statement with appropriate passages of Scripture such as Hebrews 13:56; Psalm 46 and Isaiah 43:2. A crisis tends to push God right out onto the margin of a person's life, so the first thing I attempt to do at this stage of counselling is to bring him back into the centre once again. Dr Jay Adams, Professor of Practical Theology at Westminster Theological Seminary, in the USA, puts this point most expertly when he says:

> The counsellor's task is to relate God *fully* to the crisis. It is crucial for him to re-structure the entire picture as one in which God is at work achieving His purposes for the blessing of His own, for the furtherance of the Gospel and for the honour of His Son. To do this so profoundly *changes* the crisis that it takes on an entirely new dimension. It becomes a crisis in which God is involved.

He goes on to say that when we acknowledge God as Sovereign in a crisis, then it does two things: (i) it greatly *limits* the crisis, and (ii) it gives *meaning* to it. The happenings of life are not merely tragic episodes with no point or purpose. God only allows what he can use. The counsellee needs to be shown that the crisis can, if looked at from God's point of view, contribute not to a breakdown, but to a breakthrough.

His grace is unfailing. I then seek to clarify the fact that God supplies a steady stream of grace to cope with whatever life brings us. Sometimes a counsellee says, 'I can't cope with this,' or, 'It's too much for me to bear.' Although you will sympathize with his feelings, you must bring him face to face with the fact that however he might feel, *this is not what God says*. In 1 Corinthians 10:13 God says that he will not allow one of his children to be tested above or beyond his ability to bear it. In Hebrews 12:15 the Almighty again promises that in every situation we face here on earth a constant stream of grace flows towards us, enabling us, if we receive it, to turn everything that happens to us to good account.

Don't, however, use these texts (or others) to hammer people on the head. The word of God carries its own convicting and healing power. Don't try to do God's job for him. Share this truth lovingly, gently, sensitively—but firmly.

Praise God for the problem. Here I like to read to the counsellee what I consider to be one of the most illuminating texts in the whole of the New Testament—James 1:2-3—'When all kinds of trials and temptations crowd into your lives, my brothers, don't resent them as intruders, but welcome them as friends! Realize that they come to test your faith and to produce in you the quality of endurance' (PHILLIPS).

The first time I read that text I thought it was a mistranslation, but the more I pondered it the more I realized that it contained distilled wisdom. If we fail to receive everything that happens to us with praise, then we will receive it with anger and bitterness. There is no in-between position on this. If we can't praise God for what happens to us, then we will respond with hostility. This is why, at this stage, I encourage the counsellee to purposefully praise God for what has happened to him, and to meet the crisis head on with thanksgiving.

I am aware of the debate that is currently going on in Christian circles as to whether we should praise God *for* our problems or *in spite of* our problems. Having considered both sides of the issue for many years, I am convinced that we should praise God *for* our problems, not in spite of them. When a counsellee can be brought to genuinely praise God for his problems and to see them from God's point of view, as growing points and not groaning points, then all bitterness and resentment will flow out of his spiritual system. When this happens it will not be long before a deep spiritual healing takes place.

While on this point, I draw the attention of the counsellee to consider any deficiencies in his life that may have contributed to the crisis. If there are any, then I encourage him to clear his conscience along scriptural lines. The Bible teaches that if we sin against God and against God alone, then our confession should be made only to him. If our sin involves another human being or beings, then confession should be made to God and the other person or persons concerned.

Having dealt with what I consider to be the three most important biblical truths, I then turn to any practical issues that are outstanding. Perhaps there are issues such as making an apology, restitution of goods or money, writing of letters, telephone calls to be made. Here I offer any advice that is necessary. I find it useful to draw up some kind of plan of action so that the counsellee knows what steps to take and the order in which they ought to be taken.

At this stage I see my task as completed. As all counsellors work to do themselves out of a job I encourage the counsellee (if he does not already do so) to begin to develop a close dependency on God by fencing off a part of each day for a personal 'quiet time', and using the word of God and prayer as a means to spiritual development and growth.

All that remains is to offer the counsellee the promise of my future support and to end in prayer, committing the entire situation to God. I ask that through the crisis a new awareness of God and his purposes might be made known to the counsellee, and that all future problems and emergencies might be met in the strength of the lessons that have been learned.

9

HOW TO HELP YOURSELF

or

HEY, I'M A 'PEOPLE' TOO!

Dr Gary Collins recalls sitting one day in a restaurant where the service was far from efficient. After waiting for what seemed an unusually long time, he managed to catch the waiter's attention and asked politely, 'Would you please fill my cup with coffee?' The waiter, obviously harassed and oppressed, replied somewhat curtly. 'I'll get to you soon, sir! Can't you see I have people to wait on?'

A friend sitting at Dr Collins' table, who had experienced the same inefficient service, said, 'Hey, I'm a "people" too!'

Perhaps as you have read the pages of this book, in which so far we have been focusing on the ways in which we can help others, you might have had a similar reaction. You have felt like protesting in a similar vein—'Hey, I'm a people, too.'

Well, one of the interesting things that happens whenever we set out to help others, is that invariably we finish up by helping ourselves. I'll never forget what a man said to me the other day after he had finished a week's course on the subject of 'Christian Counselling'. 'Don,' I asked, 'what have you learned about other people during this course?' This was his studied reply: 'I'm not sure what I've learned about other people, but I've been learning a lot about myself.' As I considered his reply, I began to think of the people whom I had counselled recently; many of them had reminded me of something in my own life which needed improvement. I thanked God, in those moments of reflection, for the fact that when we try to help others, more often than not we succeed in helping ourselves. As we are brought face to face with the dynamics of other people's lives, we usually begin to understand why we ourselves act the way we do. Bob, for example, had never thought much about the reasons behind people's actions, but as he became involved in counselling some of the young people in his church he began to get a clearer picture of why he himself acted and reacted as he did. This understanding led quite naturally to self-improvement and change.

It is often debated among professional counsellors whether one should try to help oneself, or whether it is best to submit one's problems to others for counselling. My own view of this issue is that when I have a personal problem which, after careful and prayerful consideration, I am not able to resolve, I believe it right and proper to share it with a trusted friend in a spirit of humility and love. I believe that if insight does not come to me direct from God, it is because he wants to use someone else in his Body to bring that insight. By so doing he ministers not only to me, but also to the one through whom the insight comes. In order to grow both psychologically and spiritually, we must be willing to receive help as well as to give it.

Having said this, however, there are many things we can do to help ourselves. In the book *A Guide to Rational Living*, the authors (Ellis & Harper) claim:

> ... it *can* be done. With or without prior psychological sophistication, an individual can read or hear about a new idea, can forcefully set about applying it to his own thought and action and can carve amazingly constructive changes in his own psyche. Not everyone can or will do this. And few of those, who, theoretically, are able to do so, actually ever will.

But some can; and some will...Let us, then, not denigrate self-analysis...

While admitting that as far as our own emotional adjustment is concerned, it is not easy, and at times not even possible, to help ourselves, what are some of the practical things we can do for a start?

1. We can learn to accept ourselves

Every one of us carries within his heart a picture of who we are and what we are like. This is what we call our 'self-concept'. If you think, 'I'm no good for anything,' 'I'm a poor husband,' or 'I'm a poor wife,' then these statements form part of your self-concept or self-image. Our self-image is important because it determines a good deal of our behaviour. Some parts of our self-image may be healthy, while other parts may be unhealthy. If a person sees himself as being a capable and efficient businessman, he will tend to function very differently from another businessman who sees himself as incapable and inefficient.

Many Christians have developed the attitude that it is right and proper to put themselves down, and they regard it as a mark of humility to debase themselves. We must see that while we are sinners and absolutely incapable of bringing about our own salvation, we are nevertheless beings created in the image of God. The Almighty values us so highly that at history's highest price, he sent his Son to be the Saviour of our souls. And because of what God has done for us, we are children of the King. We are heirs of God and joint-heirs with Christ. No one should downgrade what God has marked up as being of the highest value. To reject yourself is to disdain someone whom God loves intensely.

Self-rejection may stem from many sources. It can be the outcome of poor training in the home. A child whose parents have repeatedly downgraded him is inevitably left with a negative self-concept. He finds self-esteem difficult or even impossible. Having been always told that he is stupid or bad, he comes to believe it. Or perhaps his parents made the mistake of comparing him with a brother or sister who had more talents, or was better-looking or more likeable. If we allow past pressures of this type to determine our self-concept, we will finish up by rejecting ourselves. And if we do not learn how to accept ourselves, we will never learn how to accept others. A negative self-image will affect the whole of our life's relationships, and we will never be able to relate effectively to those whom God brings across our pathway.

Beryl was like this. She was six foot three inches tall and hated every inch of herself. She cradled within her a smouldering flame of resentment towards God and her father, both *obviously* responsible for her height. One day a friend sat down with her and showed her from Psalm 139:16 that God had a sovereign purpose in designing her the way she was: '. . . in thy book all my members were written, which in continuance were fashioned, when as yet here was none of them.' 'God had a good reason for making you the way he did,' said her friend, 'for your physical measurements are the frame of the picture God is painting on the canvas of your soul.' As Beryl listened intently she began to see, for the first time, that God had given her the right frame for the picture he was painting in her life. 'Remember,' her friend went on to say, 'a frame is designed to highlight the qualities of the painting, and God has given you the right frame to go with the picture he has prepared from all eternity to express through your life.' Once Beryl accepted herself as God designed her, she began to move towards a new and exciting dimension of living.

Your problem may lie not so much in the area of your physical appearance as in your inner mental attitudes.

Remember the famous fairy tale *Rapunzel?* It is the story of a young girl imprisoned in a tower by a wicked witch. The young girl, in fact, is very beautiful but the old witch insistently tells her that she is ugly. It is, of course, a stratagem of the witch to keep the girl in the tower. But one day her moment of liberation comes. She sees, standing at the base of the tower, her Prince Charming, and at once she lets down her long hair so that Prince Charming can braid it into a ladder and climb up to rescue her. The real imprisonment of Rapunzel is not her incarceration in the tower, but the fear of her own ugliness which the witch had so often described. However, when Rapunzel sees in the mirroring eyes of her lover that she is beautiful, she is freed from the tyranny of her own imagined ugliness.

Each one of us desperately needs to see in the mirror of another's eyes our real worth. If in the past, when looking into the mirror of other people's opinions and impressions, you have come away with a negative self-concept, then take a second look into the mirror of God's love. Learn to see yourself from God's point of view. Recognize the tremendous value God has placed upon you. Once you see that God has accepted you as you are and you are free to accept yourself in him, a new ability to relate to other people will spring up within you. Remember, your ability to relate to others depends on your ability to relate to yourself. To accept others, you must first accept yourself. I assure you that when you look into the mirror of God's love, you will like what you see.

A friend of mine, when struggling to comprehend this deeply important truth of self-acceptance, wrote out some words on a card and fixed it to his bathroom mirror, leaving it there for a month. He said it helped him more than any single thing to learn to accept himself. And what were the words? These: 'God loves you—*and so do I.*'

Recently I came across a beautiful poem by Charles Solomon which expresses the point I am trying to make.

Here it is. I hope it helps you as it helped me.

Acceptance

Oh, to know acceptance
    In a feeling sort of way;
To be known for what I am
    Not what I do or say.
It's nice to be loved and wanted
    For the person I seem to be,
But my heart cries out to be loved
    For the person who is really me!

To be able to drop all the fronts
    And share with another my fears,
Would bring such relief to my soul,
    Though accompanied by many tears.
When I find this can be done
    Without the pain of rejection,
Then will my joy be complete
    And feelings toward self know correction.

The path to feeling acceptance of God
    Is paved with acceptance on Earth;
Being valued by others I love
    Enhances my own feeling of worth.
Oh, the release and freedom he gives
    As I behold his wonderful face—
As Jesus makes real my acceptance in him,
    And I learn the true meaning of grace.

A pity it is that so late we find
    His love need not be earned;
As we yield to him all manner of strife
    A precious truth has been learned.
Then, as we share with others who search
    For love, acceptance, and rest;
They'll find in us the Saviour's love
    And experience the end of their quest.

(From Charles Solomon, *Handbook to Happiness.*)

Another way we can help ourselves and increase our effectiveness as counsellors or people-helpers is this:

2. We must work towards good mental and emotional adjustment

After reading the foregoing chapters you may have become conscious of some of the emotional problems everyone faces. The following Adjustment Rating Scale has been prepared to help you become objective about your own feelings in terms of your spiritual, mental and emotional health.

This is not a test, but as you read down the list put one tick by the side of items which sometimes present a problem to you, two ticks by those which are often a problem, and three ticks by those that are always a problem. If an item presents no problem, do not tick it at all.

Adjustment Rating Scale

I frequently become overwhelmed by my emotions (fears, anger, worries, love, etc)

I feel guilty about almost everything I do

I am always pushing myself to do more than I should

I find it hard to adjust to circumstances beyond my control

I tend to blame others for my mistakes

Sometimes I wish I had never been born

I like prestige and authority

I have great difficulty in getting over disappointments

I can't stop condemning myself for past sins

I am troubled over my lack of self-confidence

I have difficulty in working with other people

I am preoccupied with my health

I can't seem to understand what God wills for my life

My sleep is frequently disturbed

I feel nervous and apprehensive most of the time

I tend to say what I think regardless of the consequences

I have a feeling that I deserve to be punished without knowing why

My feelings are easily hurt

I act on impulse and think later

I resent being told what to do

I dislike those who disagree with me and find ways to downgrade them

I worry far more than circumstances call for

I find it difficult to take part in activities with others

I find it difficult to trust people

I do not find it easy to set realistic goals for my life

When I see a group talking, I sometimes feel they are talking
about me

I cry easily

I feel lonely even in the midst of a crowd

Most of the time I don't like myself

I feel I am too bad for God to love me

I am troubled by feelings of jealousy

I worry endlessly about the future

I feel ill at ease in meeting new people

I want more attention than I receive from those who are close
to me

I can't stand to be ignored

I become too involved with other people's problems

I sometimes feel I am losing my mind

I am afraid of God

I get nervous when I have to wait

I often feel sorry for myself

I am very critical of people I don't like

I love and hate the members of my family at the same time

I keep nursing grudges even though other people want to
make up

I am constantly concerned about my appearance

I am never satisfied with what I accomplish

I keep thinking about painful experiences I have had

I brood over mistakes of the past

I can't believe God loves me

I feel that God is punishing me for something

I doubt the truth of my own words when giving spiritual advice
to others

I often blame God for permitting things to happen in my life
the way they have

I resent criticism
I feel a failure
I often feel that God does not hear my prayers
I fear death because I don't know what will happen to me
The Bible seems no help in my problems
God seems very far away
I frequently compare myself to others who seem to have fewer
  problems
I find it difficult to refuse a request for help even when I know I
  will over-extend myself
I feel tired most of the time with no physical reason
I make unreasonable demands on myself and others
I find it difficult to give in even when I know I am wrong
I keep feeling something awful is going to happen
I am more interested in solving my own spiritual problems
  than in helping others
My home life is unhappy
I find it difficult to adjust to bad news
I would rather give orders than take them
I always seem to say the wrong thing
I find it difficult to break bad habits
When I've made a decision, I keep wondering whether or not
  I've made the right one
I put off doing things I dislike even though I know they should
  be done
I feel I need to be right always and can't stand being wrong
I find it difficult to adjust to new things and change
I allow others to manipulate me
I do not mix with people easily
I find it difficult to accept things unless they are 'perfect'
I am troubled by occasional thoughts of suicide

How did you rate? Remember, the first step to improving
your personality adjustment is to recognize your needs.
Take the items with the highest scores and begin at once
to work on them. Start with the biggest problem and bring
it before the Lord in prayer for a few days. Study the
Scriptures to see what the Bible has to say about your
problem. Buy a book that deals specifically with that issue

(or has a chapter on that issue) and explore in every way you can the solutions to your problem. Everything you do to gain a better level of personal adjustment will serve to enrich your life and make it more rewarding.

Another practical step we can take to help ourselves and thus add to our effectiveness as Christian counsellors or people-helpers is:

3. We must develop an ability to share ourselves with others

We talked earlier of the need for self-acceptance; we come now to consider the equally important concept of self-exposure. In his book *The Transparent Self* Sydney Jourard says, 'No man can come to know himself except as an outcome of disclosing himself to others.' In other words, the more we know how to share ourselves the deeper will be our own self-understanding. In some residential counsellor-training courses, would-be counsellors are encouraged to talk out with someone all their fears, apprehensions and negative feelings. There is a profound psychological and spiritual value in this. It has truly been said that we either talk out our negative feelings or we act them out. Feelings, fears and apprehensions are like steam that builds up inside a kettle. Kept inside the human system, they gather strength and blow off the lid. Repressed fears and emotions are often the cause of physical illnesses. Jourard also claims that

> illness as we know it arises in consequence of stress. Every maladjusted person is a person who has not made himself known to another human being and in consequence does not know himself. Nor can he be himself. More than that, he struggles actively to avoid becoming known by another human being. He works at it ceaselessly—twenty-four hours a day— and it is work. In the effort to avoid becoming known, a person provides for himself a cancerous kind of stress which is subtle

and unrecognised, but nonetheless effective in producing not only the assorted patterns of unhealthy personality which psychiatry talks about but also the wide array of physical ills that have come to be recognised in the province of psycho-somatic medicine.

Somewhere inside you and me lurks our real selves. There are moments when the real self shines out, but more often than not we feel compelled to camouflage it. And there is good reason for this. John Powell, in one of his books, raises the question: 'Why am I afraid to tell you who I am?' and answers it thus: 'If I tell you who I am you may not like who I am *and that is all I have got.*' It is a risky business revealing your true self to someone, for if they fail to accept you as you are you stand completely naked and exposed. Ronald, a friend of mine, found himself in this position when he joined a counsellor-training group in his church. The leader emphasized the need for self-exposure and invited the group to share themselves as authentically as they could. Ronald was the first to begin. He shared with the group just what he felt like on the inside. Taking off his mask, he let the group see what he was really like and talked about his doubts, fears and negative emotions in an open and honest manner. Two members of the group were horrified. One said, 'Ronald, I have always looked up to you as a person of deep spiritual convictions. I find it depressing to discover that on the inside this is what you are really like. You have really been deceiving us all these years.' The other person joined in at this point and said, 'Yes, that goes for me too. And what is more, if that's the kind of person you really are then I don't want anything more to do with you.' Then they both got up and walked out.

So be warned. If you see the need for self-disclosure and want to begin to share yourself and talk out your doubts, fears and apprehensions, then find someone to whom you can relate in an open and honest way, someone who will accept you as you are. Regrettably, many of our church groups and fellowships are places where people hide rather than places where they can take off their masks and say, 'This is what I am really like.' So we camouflage ourselves, wear masks, play games and pretend we are not hurting when we are.

What are the benefits of self-disclosure? They are twofold—one psychological, the other spiritual. A person who can reveal himself to others finds in the process that he empties out of himself the things that reverberate inside him when approached by people in difficulty. I can always tell a counsellor who has shared himself in this deep way because he engages in what someone called 'tensionless communication'. There is nothing inside him to reverberate when he is approached by someone with a deep problem, and this enables him to relate to that person with warmth, empathy and understanding.

The spiritual benefit is this—it enables a person to be more open in his relationship with God. Norman Grubb put it this way: imagine yourself standing in a flimsy house in which there are no doors or windows. This is your state prior to conversion. Suddenly you become converted and find that your commitment to God succeeds in blasting a hole in the roof through which you can now communicate with the Almighty. Your relationship with God, however, is limited to what goes up and what comes down to you through that one single hole. Somehow the thought grips you that outside your house there are other people you must meet and relate to, but as there are no doors or windows through which you can pass, you begin to lean on the walls which give way under your weight. This enables you to move outside and communicate with others.

As you begin to relate to others outside the now-demolished house, you find that with no walls and no roof over your head you are able to communicate with God in a far more open and unrestricted way than before. When we take the trouble to open up honest communication with our brothers and sisters in the church of Jesus Christ, we find that when we relate to God we carry over into our communication with him the honesty, openness and insights we have gained in our relationships with one another. God has designed us in such a way that the more openly we relate to one another, the more openly we will relate to him. And the more openly we relate to him, the more openly we will relate to one another. The apostle John put it this way: 'If anyone says, "I love God," but keeps on hating his brother, he is a liar; for if he doesn't love his brother who is right there in front of him, how can he love God whom he has never seen? And God himself has said that one must love not only God, but his brother too' (1 John 4:20-21 TLB).

Another way in which we can help ourselves is to take some training in the area of counselling.

To become a schoolteacher, one has to participate in a teacher-training programme. Even more training is necessary if you want to serve people in the area of dentistry, medicine, or psychiatry. Why should you not be willing to enrol in a training course if you wish to become an effective biblical counsellor? Although your own personal warmth and ability to empathize will go a long way towards making you an effective counsellor, you are unwise to rely only on them. No doubt the question is now arising in your mind: how can I as a lay person secure some training for work as a counsellor?

There are a number of organizations in the British Isles which conduct courses on the subject of counselling. Some of them, however, although they go under the umbrella of 'Christian Counselling,' are not biblically-based but rely more on psychological insights than they do on scriptural principles. The training programme in which I myself am involved is run by the Crusade for World Revival, and is in my view one of the finest biblically based counsellor-training programmes I have ever seen. Information about these courses can be obtained by contacting the Crusade for World Revival (see the end of this book).

Another way in which you can receive training is by purchasing tapes on the subject of counselling, and listening to them in company with friends who share your interest and concern. More and more cassette tapes on this subject are appearing on the market. From time to time lists of these appear in *The Christian Counsellor's Journal,* which again is published by the Crusade for World Revival. Everyone interested in the subject of counselling ought to subscribe to this volume which appears quarterly, if only to keep abreast of the aids to counsellors which are announced in its pages.

In addition to this, you can approach your minister with a view to setting up a counsellor-training programme in your church. It might be that there are a dozen or so people in the congregation who would like to work together to increase their effectiveness as counsellors. One or two could be selected to attend a residential course, and then return to share with the rest of the group the insights they have gained. I envisage over the coming years the rapid development of counselling ministries carried on by church members in almost every town, city and village of our land. Every local community of Christ's people should assume responsibility for helping distressed and discouraged people to live out their lives fully, joyfully and productively. In the past, ministers and church officials have been too eager to pass off people with personal problems to the professional helpers such as social workers, psychologists and psychiatrists. The time has come, however, when we must provide alternative resources for dealing with such personal problems within the Body of Christ. Here people can derive benefit from the tremendous healing potential that lies within a group of committed believers sharing the same faith and worshipping the same Lord.

In addressing himself to this same issue the Christian psychologist, Dr Lawrence Crabb, says. 'I suppose that some professionally trained counsellors will feel threatened by such thinking or perhaps will dismiss it as ignorant optimism. I appeal to them to consider the untapped potential for healing in the Christian community. In dealing with distressed people, counsellors who are part of the same local church and who, therefore, know the members, will be able to mobilise resources of friendship, care, practical helps and prayer in the service of their clients. In my view we professionals will still be needed but our role will change. No longer will we be the high priests of that mysterious inner world of psycho-therapy. The private practice model invites people to leave the folks who know and care for them, to go into the professional, and pay for his love and skill. In the model I am proposing, many people will turn to each other and to leaders who have been trained to find Biblical answers to their problems.'

Counselling is such serious and important work that it is worth the time and effort of preparing yourself to do it well.

Although I have left this next point until last, it should not be considered as the least valuable of my suggestions.

4. We must prepare to help ourselves as counsellors by developing a close contact and relationship with the Lord.

If you are going to make a significant and lasting contri-bution to others you must communicate the love and reality of a dynamic Christian experience. Without a vital and growing relationship with the Lord, you will be unable to deal with mankind's most pressing need—the spiritual. The keys to spiritual development are so simple that they are often overlooked.

Fence off a part of the day (preferably in the morning) when you can spend time alone with God. The psalmist said, 'In the morning my prayer comes before thee' (Psalm 88:13 RSV). Isaiah said, 'Morning by morning he wakens me and opens my understanding to his will' (Isaiah 50:4 TLB). Again, the psalmist said in Psalm 119:147, 'I am up before dawn to pray, waiting for thy promises' (Moffatt's translation). Someone said. 'If you fix your quiet time at night it will be backward-looking. If you fix it in the morning it will be forward-looking.' He did not mean, of course, that it is not necessary to pray in the evening—but the main thrust of our prayer life should be in the morning when we are most alert and at the freshest part of the day. Of course, if you cannot arrange a quiet time in the morning, you should take whatever time you can. But there can be no doubt, as thousands of Christians would testify, that the morning is best.

> Every morning lean thine arm awhile
> Upon the window sill of heaven
> And gaze upon thy God,
> Then with the vision in thy heart
> Turn strong to meet the day.

Spend time each day in reading and meditating upon God's word. A Christian counsellor cannot afford to neglect his Bible. The Bible contains, as no other book does, the thoughts of Almighty God. This is why it is sometimes difficult to understand, for his thoughts are higher than our thoughts and his ways higher than our ways. As our thoughts and natural inclinations are directly contrary to God's principles, we must seek to rearrange our thought structures within the framework of God's will. By reading and meditating on the word of God, we expose our thoughts to his thoughts so that quietly and gently his thoughts mingle with ours and help to reconstruct our thinking. This positively affects our emotions.

As we read God's word, the Bible, and allow his thoughts to infiltrate ours, we condition our mind to think as God thinks; for perusal of his word is really *thinking God's thoughts after him.* The more we expose ourselves to his thoughts, the more we will be able to think like God and have his mind working in ours. When we give our minds to him, he gives his mind to us and reconstructs our thought patterns within the framework of his divine purposes. In this way, Scripture leaps up and takes on a new and fresh meaning. Familiar words shine with a new light. It is never enough to say that God has spoken through the Scriptures. *He speaks through them still.*

Learn to walk in the Spirit. There are thousands of people who have committed their lives to Jesus Christ but who have never grown spiritually. They stay spiritual infants and, like Peter Pan, they never grow up. Make sure you are not one of them.

Paul says in Galatians 5:16, 'This I say then, walk in the Spirit, and ye shall not fulfil the lust of the flesh.' We hear a great deal these days about being baptized in the Spirit, filled with the Spirit, empowered by the Spirit; but not much about walking in the Spirit. All these other aspects of the Spirit-filled life are equally important, of course, but let's focus for a few moments on what *walking in the Spirit* really means.

It means watching where you walk, treading carefully through life so that you keep avoiding the things which Paul lists in this chapter: 'impure thoughts, eagerness for lustful pleasure, idolatry, spiritism (that is, encouraging the activity of demons), hatred and fighting, jealousy and anger, constant effort to get the best for yourself, complaints and criticisms, the feeling that everyone else is wrong except those in your own little group...wrong doctrine, envy, murder, drunkenness, wild parties, and all that sort of thing' (Galatians 5:19-21 TLB).

If we are walking in the Spirit, we will walk *away* from these things. Paul, however, gives another list of things which he calls the fruit of the Spirit. These are things not to walk away from, but things to walk towards. The experience of walking in the Spirit is not the result of some ecstatic feeling you might have had at some time in your past, but a daily act of commitment in which you decide to walk God's way and allow his Holy Spirit to control your thinking, your emotions and your decisions.

10

DANGERS TO AVOID
IN PEOPLE-HELPING

Doctors of medicine classify certain ailments as 'occupational diseases'. The miner, for example, is prone to pneumoconiosis and nystagmus. Lead painters are prone to colic. Quarrymen become subject to silicosis. Men who work at these kinds of jobs fall prey to such ailments because they are endemic to that calling. Surprising as it may appear to some, the work of Christian counselling has its occupational diseases as well. Not everyone succumbs to them, and not all are attacked, but it is imperative that we know where the dangers lie and be on our guard against them.

Some of these dangers are not peculiar to the work of a counsellor. They are part of fallen human nature, something we share with every other being in the universe; but they may come upon a counsellor with peculiar force by reason of what he does and the circumstances under which he does it.

1. Over-curiosity

Sometimes in a counselling situation a counsellor will temporarily forget the needs of the counsellee and begin probing for information designed to satisfy his own curiosity. Tom, a good friend of mine, was like this.

Whenever he found himself counselling a married man who had problems in his marriage, he would probe unnecessarily into this person's sex life. There are times when a counsellor is obliged to explore this area, but more often than not it is unnecessary. When a counsellee complained to me that Tom invariably brought the conversation round to sexual matters, I spoke to him about it. He was quite unaware that this was a trend in his counselling approach. When I shared with him my opinion that his own sexual inadequacy (a matter we had previously talked about) seemed to be pushing him to the edge of voyeurism, he thanked me profusely. A counsellor must be alert to any tendencies within himself that motivate him towards becoming over-curious, and discipline himself to avoid taking the conversation too far in that direction.

Be aware of your weak points and learn to rely on the Holy Spirit to help you when you are tempted to become over-curious.

2. Sexual attraction

Some counsellors, by reason of their position, training and experience, find themselves having to counsel members of the opposite sex. And sometimes sexual stimulation can take place without its being intended, or without either person being aware of what is happening. This can work in both directions (from the counsellor to the counsellee and vice versa). A woman I once counselled over a period of several weeks came into the counselling room on the first occasion, took off her coat and hung it up. At the end of the session, as she was about to leave, I reached for her coat and helped her on with it. After a few sessions of counselling I sensed that my helping her with her coat at the end of the session was beginning to be misinterpreted. I came to this conclusion because of the unusually long time she took to put her arms into the coat and button it up. I raised the point tactfully with her, and she admitted that she was developing a great liking for this attention. I shared with her the danger both to her and to myself that could arise if this was not talked out, faced and dealt with.

Women have been a source of temptation to men ever since time began, and some men feel temptation more strongly than others. We are especially prone to temptation when we are convinced that it cannot come. A male counsellor who puts his arm round a woman counsellee in order to comfort her may not realize that she might misinterpret his demonstration of affection. There are times when it is right to do this, and there are times when it is wrong. Each one of us must develop a deep spiritual sensitivity so that we can follow the dictates of the Holy Spirit at each given moment of our lives.

3. A sense of superiority

There is a danger in all callings and professions of being superior and overbearing, but such an attitude always seems especially heinous when it creeps into the ministry of people-helping. Unless one is careful, the insights gained concerning the way people think and behave can contribute to a sense of superiority arising within one's soul. I remember being counselled as a teenager by a man who had great experience in counselling, and who was widely known in the area where I lived for his expertise and skill. Never, as long as I live, will I forget the negative impression he made on me. His latent sense of superiority infected his whole manner, and he talked down to me in a way that I bitterly resented. The language he used, psychological words and phrases that I had never heard before, went right over my head. His judgement on my problem came over with such a hardness that I cried. He did not see the courage with which I stood up to other problems in my life. The man was learned, experienced, and highly trained. But he was utterly out of touch with life, and utterly unaware of it.

If, during your counselling experiences, you find that there arises in you a sense of superiority—then squash it the way you would squash a louse.

4. A leak of confidence

While it is true that a lay counsellor is not legally bound by the same confidentiality code that is so important to professionals, the same principle applies—never share information shared with you by a counsellee without the counsellee's permission. If, in the course of counselling, you feel it necessary that something said or done should be shared with someone else, then tell the counsellee why it would benefit him for that information to be shared. In all my experience with thousands of people over the past thirty years, I have never once known a counsellee resist my suggestion to share information with someone else, after having shown him that it was in his best interests to do so.

5. Jumping to conclusions

When I first started counselling as a pastor, a woman came to me complaining bitterly about her husband. She told me he was mean, cruel, unspiritual, unloving, and a rogue. My immediate reaction was this—just wait until the next time I see him, he will certainly get a piece of my mind! When I met the husband later I told him exactly what I thought of him. He listened patiently, then told me the situation *from his point of view*. I remember being taken aback, for I realized that I had made my first big mistake—I had jumped too hastily to conclusions. Every one of us describes events, circumstances and problems *as we see them*—from our own point of view. In counselling we usually hear one side of the issue—the counsellee's. More often than not this is only one side of the matter. In some counselling situations, particularly marriage counselling, one needs to get the views of others who are involved so that the picture can be brought into its proper perspective.

6. Over-activity

Over-activity is not a peril only for the counsellor, but here again we meet it in a special way. Occasionally I meet counsellors who are so busy meeting other people's needs that they are seriously in danger of needing counselling themselves. Christian counselling is, in many ways, nervously exhausting. There is a physical expenditure which has spiritual consequences. If a counsellor persists in seeing one person after another without making time for relaxation and recuperation, he may soon find himself spent.

A counsellor in this position must plainly recognize that if his body is not having its due, then he is in danger of sinning against himself. He should aim to walk each day and to learn how to relax. The mind must rest from spiritual problems and be occupied with things of a far less serious nature.

7. Seeing truth as something only others need

Here a peculiar peril of the counsellor appears. It is the peril of sharing biblical truths and principles by knowledge rather than by experience. Carlyle, speaking of the tendency of preachers to utter truths from their heads rather than from their hearts, said, 'It is a sad but rare truth that every time you speak of a fine purpose, especially if with eloquence, and to the admiration of by-standers, there is the less chance of your ever making a fact of it in your own poor life.' How awful! This is an occupational disease indeed. Lloyd George said of Briand in the first world war, 'As soon as Briand descended from the rostrum he took no further interest in his speeches. For him, speech was the same thing as action. At least, his contribution ended with his perorations; it was for others to do the rest. If they neglected to do so, he was not to blame...' (*War Memoirs of David Lloyd George,* Ivor Nicholson and Watson, pp.2, 334f.).

What can a counsellor do about this danger of sharing biblical truth as a purveyor of principles rather than through his own personal experience? I can only share my own humble testimony. Long aware of this danger, I have tried to incorporate into my own life every biblical principle I share with others. Prior to a counselling session, when I know I will need to present some biblical insight to bring about a solution to a person's problem, I try to make that truth autobiographical. I try to live in it, to incarnate in my own life the truth I feel led to share; to know the thing in experience before I utter it in words. It is not always possible to achieve this, of course, but, believe me, I *try!*

8. A wrong emphasis

Many *professional* Christian counsellors, such as psychiatrists and psychologists, consider that the two greatest weaknesses of lay counsellors are an over- and under-use of spiritual resources. Some Christians are of the opinion that all that is necessary for effective counselling is reading the Bible and saying a prayer. It is true, of course, that there *are* occasions when this is precisely all that is needed, and one must come to terms with this. At the other end of the scale are the counsellors who ignore prayer and the Scriptures and rely exclusively on the use of psychological techniques.

To some extent, the right approach will be determined by the nature of the problem. A grief-stricken widow could be greatly comforted by an appropriate Scripture passage and a word of prayer, whereas a depressed person would benefit more from the sharing of a useful insight before turning to the word and prayer. To assume that *all* problems should be handled by prayer and the reading of the Scriptures is as naïve as assuming that there is no place for the Bible in counselling. The right balance between these two things can mean the difference between success and failure in a counsellor's experience.

9. A sense of failure

Not all counselling sessions end successfully. Sometimes, despite our best efforts, we just don't seem to get anywhere. At such times a counsellor must be on his guard not to allow a seemingly unsuccessful interview filch his spiritual peace. Jesus knew what it was like to have a counselling session produce no results. The rich young ruler, when confronted by Christ with the fact that his riches were the main focus of his life, turned and walked away. Obviously Christ did not fall apart in such a situation. He showed sorrow when the young man walked away, but he did not blame himself by saying, 'I might have won that young man if I had put things differently.' No one (apart from Jesus, of course) is perfect, and we must learn to see failure in its right perspective. A counsellor can share, explain, pray, read the Scriptures, warn, admonish, encourage, direct; but he cannot make a person *obey*. If a counsellor feels he has failed in his approach to a person, then he is responsible not for the counsellee's actions or failure to improve, but for taking the steps he knows to be necessary so that he will not make the same mistake again.

Sometimes the question is raised, 'But what if a counsellee goes out and commits suicide? How do I handle that?' Jesus, you remember, faced this problem also. Judas, a member of his own team, committed suicide. If a counsellee gives up on God, on himself and on everyone else and commits suicide, then the *counsellee alone* bears that responsibility. Any counsellor would deeply regret having a counsellee commit suicide, but it is quite wrong for a counsellor to carry the guilt of such an action.

10. Laziness

Laziness is something which can tempt people in all callings, but again the ministry of counselling puts the peril in its own peculiar way. Here is the subtlety of it—a man can be lazy at counselling without going too frequently to the golf course or some other form of recreation. He can delude himself that he is preparing for a counselling session when in fact he is idling away the hours, fiddling a few papers or indulging his imagination in some juicy piece of gossip, instead of seeking to add to his effectiveness by reading, prayer, or study.

Schedule your life so that you can listen to a tape, read a new book, or think through some new insight for counselling. Guard these minutes. The hours will take care of themselves.

11. A desire for acceptance

The desire for acceptance can be a real peril to a counsellor. Unless he has learned how to meet in God his need for acceptance, he will find himself turning to a counselling interview in order to achieve it. This desire for acceptance, if not focused on God, can seduce a counsellor in many ways. He can become more interested in saying something new than something true. He may use devices, clutching at any modern technique or the latest psychological insight, in order to make an impression. He will aim to be smart, rather than deep; profound rather than discerning; brilliant rather than helpful; interesting rather than effective.

No counsellor will ever experience fulfilment and meaning in his life by the simple recollection that someone he has counselled believes him to be a person of importance.

12. Jealousy and envy

I almost shrink from mentioning this, but it has to be faced. Perhaps it would shock a counsellee if he knew we had this to grapple with. A counsellee expects secular counsellors to be jealous of each other—but Christian counsellors! Is it possible? It is not only possible, it is actual. It sometimes arises when a counsellee says, 'I was greatly helped some time ago by another Christian counsellor, brother or sister so and so, who seemed to have the knack of seeing right through me and showing me how to put things right.' Sometimes (not always) when this happens one feels stirrings within that can only be described as jealousy and envy. Lord, have mercy on us!

Jealousy arises from a wrong comparison. At some level of our mental and emotional life we seem to pose the question to ourselves, 'What has he got that I haven't got?' When faced by a counsellee who has nothing but praise for another counsellor who has greatly helped him, we know that we ought to praise that counsellor too. But we usually end up doing it grudgingly and with a flavour of disappointment: 'Yes, he does seem to have a good reputation. I understand he has some family problems of his own, though....' Just a nuance. But a discerning counsellee will not miss it...and will wonder at the cause. No counsellor is really free until he is free of this.

13. Personal admiration

The last and most clear of our occupational diseases is the danger we are in from people who admire us because they have got the help of Christ in our counselling. We can understand it happening, but we must not pander to it. A counsellee comes to share a problem that perhaps has been with him for years. Low-spirited, discouraged, and expectant, he sits before you hanging on your every word. And God bends to his need: gives you the word that nourishes his soul, lifts the depression right out of him, and sends him back to his family radiant. How can he help but be glad and appreciative? Is it surprising that he might confuse the Source and the channel?

Sometimes a person who has been greatly helped will come to you again, pouring out his expression of thanks as if it were you, not God, who has given him help. It is not easy to set about 'correcting' everyone who is grateful. One can say, 'It was not me but God who helped you,' but that sounds a little pedantic, and perhaps a little pedagoguish also. No, the best way by far is to accept the gratitude and bring it to God along with your own thanks. 'God,' said someone, 'will always delight in his servant's discernment, and take the thanks of his people at second hand.'

Of course, the real peril in this arises from the possibility that a counsellor supposes the thanks *belongs* to him, and receives it from people as a right. He may regard it as a tribute to his own training, insight, and experience, and come to look for it and live on it.

The sovereign way to avoid this peril, and indeed all others, is a life of intimate communion with God.

11

SEVEN STEPS
TO EFFECTIVE LIVING

At almost any point in time you are probably close to someone who is in desperate need of spiritual help. Someone in your home, school, office, factory, shop, or church may be hurting over a husband who is unfaithful, a daughter who is defiant and immoral, or a job that is in jeopardy, or experiencing feelings of inner guilt and emptiness. Some are depressed; some are despairing. Some feel that even though they pray about their problems there is no one there. Whatever one's beliefs may be, or whatever commitment one has to the Lord Jesus Christ, no one is exempt from internal battles, emotional hurts and painful problems. So there is great need for erecting a ladder that helps us climb out of our difficulties. Such a ladder I want to present to you now. Start to climb it yourself if you are in difficulty, and then share the truths with those who need help.

1. Accept the fact that God loves you

I realize that some may have difficulty in accepting this fact, but it is the very first rung on the ladder to effective living. Mike, a 28-year-old schoolteacher, came to me for counselling and described his problem in these words: 'I believe the Bible is true and I know that when it says God loves me it is a definite fact, but for some reason I am not able to accept it as a reality in my life and experience. I never knew love in my childhood, and I'm wondering whether this is hindering my perception and understanding of God's love as it is expressed and explained in the Bible.' I said, 'Mike, the phrase you used, "I never knew love in my childhood," is probably the key to the whole problem.' I went on to explain to Mike that we all start life in a position of dependency, needing to *be* loved. Our sense of God's love is rigidly conditioned by our experience of being loved by our parents. If parental love has been spasmodic and conditional, then naturally we expect God's love to be spasmodic and conditional. If our parents were over-indulgent with their love, then we expect God to be over-indulgent with his love. If our parents were punitive and restrictive, then we come to see God in this way, and the sense of his love is likewise distorted.

Long experience in dealing with someone who finds it difficult to accept the fact of God's love because of deprivation in childhood has shown me that, more often than not, this leaves a lingering bitterness within the personality. I asked Mike how he felt towards his parents at the present moment and he said, 'I have no bitterness against them for their lack of love towards me, and things are fine between us now.' I felt uneasy with his answer, and gently probed into his past until we came to an experience Mike had when he was aged ten. He had been selected to play in the junior boys' football team and, wishing to impress his father with his skill as a footballer, begged him to come and watch him play. At the football match, towards the end of the 90-minute period, Mike scored the winning goal. As the crowd cheered he looked towards the stands to where he knew his father was sitting —only to discover that he had left early and gone home.

As Mike recounted this story I saw his lip quiver and a tear start in his eye. Gently and tactfully, I suggested to him that in the hurt and pain of that memory might linger an unrecognized and unconfessed bitterness. He responded positively to this suggestion and asked me to help him locate and remove any bitterness which might be lingering in his personality. As we talked, it became obvious that despite his earlier statement that he felt no bitterness towards his father, deep down within his personality—below the level of consciousness—were suppressed feelings of resentment that were now coming to the surface. In prayer we bundled these together and brought them to the cross. Mike asked God's forgiveness for his previously unrecognized resentments, and having got them out he experienced a great sense of release. 'What happens now?' was his next question.

'Well,' I said, 'now that you have got rid of your inner resentments against your father for the deprivations of your childhood, you are ready to open yourself in a new way to the fact that God loves you. You see, until we get rid of bitterness and resentment God is unable to reveal himself to us in the way he desires' (this point is discussed in greater detail later on in the chapter). I went on to show Mike that the truth of God's love is not simply a theory, but a proven fact. 'God loves you,' I said, 'and the proof of that love is Jesus Christ. Christian scholars such as Pascal and C. S. Lewis suggest that the evidence of God's love is not to be found in nature, for while people talk about seeing the love of God in beautiful sunsets and in the autumn colours, they must also face the facts of animals tearing each other to pieces, of tornadoes, floods and famines. Nature may reveal the greatness and power of God, but it is difficult to prove from nature that God is love. The ultimate proof that God loves us is in the person of Jesus Christ. Here is God's great identification with us. He became like us in order to make us like himself. At the cross he agonized and died to save us from our sin. When we come to that cross and gaze at the divine self-sacrifice,

156

we see the love of God in a way that is impossible to deny. Seeing Christ on the cross as God's proof that he loves us is the most powerful way I know of coming to terms with the fact that God loves you. Let's pray together now and ask the Lord to make his love real to you.'

As Mike opened his heart in prayer to the Lord and asked God to make his love real to him, the Holy Spirit came to him in a very special way. He told me later that he sensed he was in the presence of God, that God loved him and that through Christ he was as dear to God as his own beloved Son.

If you find it difficult to accept the fact that God loves you, first ask God to heal the scars of old experiences of rejection, and make sure that you are holding no bitterness towards anyone who has hurt or wronged you. Then focus your thoughts as long and as often as you can on the truth that the most convincing evidence of God's love is the fact that he gave his Son to die for your sin. Ask the Lord to make this real to you. Soon you should be able to revel in this as a solid fact, and go on to fully experience in your life its healing and uplifting power.

2. Face your problems and don't hide from a single one

This is the first law of psychological health—admit your problems. It is quite amazing the lengths to which people will go in order to avoid facing their problems. Many Christians suffer much more than they need to by denying they have problems, when deep down inside they know they have. Some Christians have the idea that if anyone has a problem he can't be a very good Christian. So what happens? Instead of admitting they have a problem they repress it—put a lid on it and push it down into the unconscious. They don't seem to know that one of the laws of the unconscious is that it can't keep anything to

itself. Repressed conflicts will come out—either as illnesses in the body or as wrong patterns of behaviour.

It's not easy, of course, to face our problems and look at
what is going on inside us. It's much better, we believe, to
hide behind a smiling face and put on a respectable front, or
even a discreet silence. Eric Berne wrote a book which has
become a best seller, called *Games People Play*. In it he
shows the kind of things people get up to in an attempt to
conceal themselves and keep others from seeing them as
they really are. One day I hope to write a book or article on
this same subject and call it *Games Christians Play*.

One of the games Christians play is what I have chosen
to call 'Heads, I win—tails, you lose.' This is when we
pray for the pride, arrogance, conceit and self-centredness
in others while feigning innocence, unawareness of the
same, or similar, things in ourselves. It works like this,
too: 'It's all right for me to gossip, but don't you dare
smoke.' Or, 'It's fine for me to point out the deficiencies in
the pastor, but don't ever let me hear you say that my
interpretation of Scripture is wrong.'

Another game Christians play is called 'Let God do it'.
A woman who had great difficulty in relating to other
people in her church was challenged about the issue by
her pastor. 'I'll let God take care of it,' was her reply. The
minister showed her that she was really playing games
with God, expecting him to do something he had already
done—give her the ability to relate, share and develop
meaningful relationships with others.

Yet another game Christians play is called 'Let's gossip
while we pray': 'I think we should really pray for David
and Betty,' said one person in a crowded prayer meeting,
'I think they are having marital problems, and may be
heading for divorce.' Sounds like a normal, caring
interest, doesn't it? It isn't. It's a game. David and Betty
may, like most married couples, be experiencing
problems. But to have the fact advertised in a church

prayer meeting is hardly right and proper. The informant was simply indulging in a juicy bit of gossip.

Each one of us needs to resist firmly this tendency to avoid looking at ourselves and facing our inner problems. 'Is it not ironic,' says Dr James Mallory, a Christian psychiatrist, 'that when a person has a salvation experience he very honestly opens himself up to Jesus Christ, confessing his sin and revealing himself in his great need but, as he goes further in his Christian experience, he often begins to "fake it instead of make it". He does not maintain this honesty and openness and is not walking in the light anymore.'

Don't hide from your problems. Face them in the certainty that God loves you as you are, and is not ashamed when he sees you have a problem.

3. Assume personal responsibility for the way you are

Another step on the ladder to effective Christian living is to acknowledge that it is not so much what happens to you as what you do with it that matters. People blame society, their parents, and even God for what happens to them, forgetting that with the right inner attitudes every setback can become a springboard, and every stumbling block a stepping stone. We are not responsible for what happens to us, but we are responsible for the way we respond to what happens to us.

A man told me on one occasion, 'I can't be blamed for the way I am, because in the weaving of my personality pattern on the loom of life I was hurt, injured, ridiculed and scorned, probably more than anyone.' I pointed out to him that when the shuttle of circumstances, events and attitudes was passed to him through that loom, he was faced with the choice of whether to return it in the way it was given (with bitterness and recrimination) or to pass it back in a spirit of love, forgiveness and consideration.

Unfortunately, many modern psychologists have contributed to the idea that people are not really responsible for what they do. 'Your mother didn't love you,' they say, 'and so you have deep complexes from which it will take a long time to recover.' Whatever happened to us in the past, if we really wanted to we could have responded differently. As long as we blame circumstances or others, we lose sight of the fact that 'in Christ' we can be set free from every bondage of the past, every wrong attitude, and every negative emotion.

A song by Anna Russell expresses today's syndrome of people who are not prepared to accept personal responsibility for their behaviour.

> I went to my psychiatrist
>   to be psychoanalysed
> To find out why I killed the cat
>   and blackened my wife's eyes.
>
> He put me on a downy couch
>   To see what he could find,
> And this is what he dredged up
>   From my subconscious mind:
>
> When I was one, my mummy hid
>   My dolly in the trunk
> And so it follows naturally
>   That I am always drunk.
>
> When I was two, I saw my father
>   Kiss the maid one day
> And that is why I suffer now—
>   Kleptomania.
>
> When I was three, I suffered from
>   Ambivalence towards my brothers,
> So it follows naturally,
>   I poisoned all my lovers.

> I'm so glad that I have learned
> The lesson it has taught,
> That everything I do that's wrong
> Is someone else's fault.

There is very little hope that we can climb out of the pit of despair and discouragement if we don't take the responsibility for ourselves and say, 'All right, so life has been cruel and unkind to me. But others have been faced with the same problems that I face, and some of them have reacted differently. By their right attitudes they have turned their pain into a pearl. So will I. With Christ in my life I will use his power to forgive everyone who has hurt me, transform every trial into a testimony, and make every difficulty a discovery.'

Things that strike into our lives make us bitter—or better, according to the way we respond. As a plane takes off against the rising wind, so can you, strengthened by Christ, rise above every adversity to a new vision of God and his glory.

4. Forgive everyone who has ever hurt you

We saw this principle briefly illustrated in the case of Mike, earlier in this chapter, but we will now discuss it in greater detail. No one can afford to carry a grudge. It takes too much toll. A Welsh proverb says that you chew on your own tongue when you chew on resentment. As long as we harbour an unforgiving spirit we cannot expect to climb out of the pit of discouragement and despair. This is a principle that Christ made clear in his sermon on the mount: 'For if you forgive men when they sin against you, your heavenly Father will also forgive you. But if you do not forgive men their sins, your Father will not forgive your sins' (Matthew 6:14-15, New International Version). As you stand in need of forgiveness, so give it to others.

For if you refuse it to others, this blocks the forgiveness of God towards you. God cannot forgive the unforgiving. His hands are tied. If we refuse forgiveness we break down the bridge over which we must pass—the bridge of forgiveness.

The highest statement of morality ever given on this planet of ours is this one: 'Treat one another with the same spirit as you experience in Christ Jesus' (Philippians 2:5, Moffatt). Treat each other the way Christ treats you. He forgives and he forgives freely; he forgets and he forgets wholly; he buries and he buries completely.

Many Christians find it hard to recognize and identify resentment as an evil thing, because it is so skilful in justifying itself. People believe that if resentment is justified they may *legitimately* hold it. Indeed, some would go as far as to say they *ought* to hold it and that it would be foolish and weak *not* to hold it. Let's make no mistake about this, as to take a wrong step here will be fatal. It is not the naturalness of resentment that is important, but the poison that flows through the emotion. Legitimate or not, it is a parasite in the mind. The evil germ is in the mind of the man who entertains it, not in the mind of the man who caused it.

Dr William Edwin Sangster says in one of his books,

I knew a man whose young and lovely wife was killed by a drunken motorist. That desolate man was left to face the world alone with twin children—a boy and a girl. That he should be broken in sorrow for a while, everybody understood, but when the shock had passed and the edge had come off his grief, he burned with a concentrated hatred against his wife's murderer. Always (and not without justification) he referred to the drunken motorist as the 'murderer'. His home grew darker and darker. He became a sullen recluse. The children felt they had not only lost their mother, but their father also. And they had. There were senses in which he had died as much as his wife had done, but there lived in his place a morose monster of whom the children grew half afraid. There was no cure for that much-injured man, and no recovery of his health, until he came to the point of forgiveness and sought the healing of this awful sorrow in God.

Far too many Christians are avid injustice collectors. This is a deliberate disobedience of God's law of love. To know freedom and deliverance we must bring out into the light every feeling of resentment and injustice, nail them to the cross of Christ and be made whole.

7. Avoid self-pity

It would be hard to exaggerate the dangers of self-pity. That a man should look so long and intently at his troubles that he becomes a martyr to them, is one of the most distressing conditions into which a human being can fall. What causes people to succumb to self-pity? Is it just a question of temperament? Were they born melancholic, and will they remain that way until they die?

Sensitive people, we find, are most prone to self-pity. This is because they are easily hurt. Unless they recognize that their sensitivity is a capacity for sympathy and that their ability to feel deeply is really God's equipment to feel deeply for others, they will become trapped into a miserable mood of complaint, and whine and whimper their days away. Self-pity turns molehills into mountains. Trivialities assume tremendous proportions. Inconveniences become great trials. A man or woman obsessed with self-pity can pass through a hospital ward filled with the bodies of those suffering from the direst diseases, and come out complaining of a slight headache. The whole set of their thinking and the emotional tone of their life-style is blue, and everything dipped into it comes out with that dye. When the weather is hot they wish it were cold. When it is cold, they wish it were hot. They study all events to find a dark side. If they cannot find it, they invent it.

But how do we overcome it? What steps can we take to rid ourselves of this ugly weed in our soul? Self-pity is an emotion—a capacity to feel things and to feel them deeply. The word emotion implies a movement *outwards*. Pity, therefore, should go to others. When we keep our eyes on Christ and try to follow his example, we will catch sight of the fact that living as we do in a love-hungry and pity-provoking world, it is not *Christian* to expend pity on ourselves. Keep in mind that pity is perverted when it is turned inward and becomes self-pity.

The secret, then, of overcoming self-pity is a mind that is centred on God and on his Son Jesus Christ. With this attitude all the hard disciplines of life can be accepted with courage and, through God's love, be turned to advantage. To moan about life's seeming misfortunes dishonours God by implying that he is mismanaging his world and doesn't care about what happens to his creation. Begin to unselfishly turn your sensitivity to sympathy and compassion for others. Radiate good cheer, thrust your shoulder under someone else's burden, and learn of the joy that comes through serving the King of kings.

6. Discipline your mind

You will no doubt recall that in one chapter of this book I argued that erroneous beliefs are to blame for the negative emotions of resentment, guilt and anxiety. Wrong assumptions about life produce wrong feelings, which in turn produce wrong behaviour. Scripture emphasizes over and over again that what a person thinks and believes is central to effective functioning. We are *transformed*, says the great apostle Paul, not merely by attempting to bring about a change in our feelings or in our behaviour, but by the 'renewing of our minds'. In Romans 12:1-2 Paul beseeches us not to be conformed to the world (a false and untrue system), but to be transformed by the renewing of our minds. Consider carefully what this implies.

(1) It is possible to believe in a false and untrue system; in other words, to believe a lie.

(2) There is a true system to which God wants me to conform.

(3) If I am to live the kind of life God wants me to live on his earth, then it becomes necessary to think the right kind of thoughts.

Listen to what Paul says in another part of the New Testament: 'This, I say therefore, and testify in the Lord, that ye henceforth walk not as other Gentiles walk, in the vanity of their mind, having the understanding darkened, being alienated from the life of God through the ignorance that is in them, because of the blindness of their heart' (Ephesians 4:17-18). Wrong thinking leads to wrong feeling, and wrong feeling leads to wrong behaving.

Under the lordship of Jesus Christ we can actually counter the mind-set which has been produced by our carnal nature and insist on thinking God's thoughts after him. For example, if someone criticizes us we can direct our minds to pay attention to God's word for this situation, which will point out to us that 'all things work together for good'—even criticism. Because we know from those matchless verses in Romans 8:28-29 that God uses everything to make us more like his son, Jesus Christ, we can respond to the situation with praise (positive emotion) and serve the Lord (right behaviour) in the way that truly glorifies him.

When we decide that we are going to think thoughts that are based on God's principles, a new dimension of living opens up before us. We will view every person, every circumstance, and every situation as an opportunity to experience the development of Christ's character within us. So many Christians think in a manner totally contrary to this; people, circumstances, and situations are a threat and a burden to them. So decide now that you will not be a poor-mouth Christian and talk yourself out of God's blessings for your life. Remember, you are not what you think you are, but what you think—you are!

7. Meet every situation that comes your way with praise

Listen to what Paul said in 1 Thessalonians 5:17—'Always be thankful no matter what happens' (TLB). Even though we may not like the circumstances in which we find ourselves we can legitimately praise God for them, resting in the knowledge that ultimately all things work together for good to them that love God.

A friend of mine who is a minister tells how in one church he pastored, although there was great blessing in many areas of the church, some serious undercurrents surfaced one day in a church business session. He says he would not have known how to respond to that situation were it not for the fact that earlier in his life he had attended a ministers' seminar in which the principle of praising God for all things had been explained and expounded.

He said, 'I began to thank God for the opposition. This was my starting point. Hard? Definitely, but immensely important. The clear scriptural instruction to thank God in all things is far more important and essential than many of us realize, for it puts in motion the necessary inward attitudes to creatively view an experience from God's perspective. We often see conflict as an interruption to a church programme, when in actuality it is a continuing process for personal growth.'

Listen again to this gripping truth: '*Thanking God in all things puts in motion the necessary inward attitudes to creatively view the experience from God's perspective.*' Can you see what he means? When we respond to all of life's situations with praise and gratitude to God, it prevents our spirits from becoming soured and enables us to see life from God's point of view.

The psalmist says in Psalm 34:1, 'I will bless the LORD at all times: his praise shall continually be in my mouth.' Can we really be expected to praise the Lord at all times? *Some* times, perhaps. Or *most* times. Or even *almost* all the time. Not so, says the psalmist: 'I will bless the LORD at all times.' Bad times. Good times. Down times. Up times. In times. Out times...his praise shall continually be in my mouth. However difficult is your path through life (and believe me, I am not unmindful of this) make up your mind to follow the advice of the psalmist and fill your days with unceasing praise. 'But,' I almost hear you say, 'with so many pressing problems and difficulties crowding my path, I can find nothing to be really thankful for.' Well, begin by thinking on the wonder of the fact that you, a soiled sinner, can find a welcome in the presence of a Holy God, and that you can *linger* in his presence as long as you like. Contemplate the fact also that God is the true owner of the universe and the world is not (as some think) the sporting arena of half-mad men. God is in control of everything that happens, and he will not allow anyone to take from you anything that contributes to your spiritual loss. It may seem at times that God permits others to deprive you, but he is in it all, permitting only what he sees will accord with his purpose. *The loss he turns to gain.* So focus your mind on the fact that in everything that happens to us there is more to praise than we first thought. Learn to praise him not just some times, or most times, but at *all* times.

12

PUTTING IT ALL TOGETHER

In order to pull together many of the insights and principles I have dealt with in this book, I think it might be helpful if I present for you a typical counselling session in which a Christian counsellor, using a combination of spiritual truths and psychological principles, attempts to help a person in distress.

In counselling, as indeed in other areas of life, we learn best by looking at practical examples. I hope the example that follows, based on the model presented in chapter 6, will enable you to comprehend how a biblical counsellor proceeds to help a person reach that important goal of counselling—helping a person become more like Jesus Christ. Before you read the account of this interview, I feel it right to say that it is a condensed and compacted version of what really takes place in an in-depth counselling encounter. A much longer time would normally be given to history-taking and evaluating the problem. It should also be noted that not all counselling is as straightforward and as simple as this case appears to be. Sometimes a counsellee can dodge down a side road from which it is difficult to extricate him. The model is included here to help you see something of the direction in which a counsellor moves when confronted by a serious problem.

The interview is between a man named Bill and an

unnamed counsellor. The counsellor's private thoughts are set in brackets.

Counsellor: 'Hello, Bill. Good to see you. Sit down and share with me your problem. What seems to be the trouble?'

Bill: 'I'm really not sure. I feel depressed all the time. When I wake up in the morning I feel as if I haven't been to sleep. Everything I do seems to be an effort. It's as if there's a steel band round my head that I can't get rid of.'

Counsellor: 'Sounds like you're having a pretty difficult time.' (I'd like to explore what's wrong, but at this stage it would be too threatening. I'll just let Bill talk and try to establish a relationship.) 'Tell me some of the other ways your depression affects you.'

Bill: 'Well, I've given up reading the Bible and although I do try to pray, it seems as if God is far away and doesn't listen to me. I guess my spiritual life is pretty low at the moment.'

Counsellor: (Bill is obviously hurting. I need to show him that I genuinely care about the way he is feeling, non-verbally as well as verbally. I'll lean forward, towards him a little, and at the same time try to build a bridge of communication between us by identifying and labelling his feelings.) 'I know from my own experience and from talking with others, Bill, that when depression hits it can be pretty devastating. Someone described it like walking into your own home at night and searching for the light switch, which you have done a thousand times before, but you find it isn't there. You go into the other rooms and find that somehow all the switches have disappeared. Is that how you feel?'

Bill: 'Yes, that's it exactly. How long do I have to stay like this? Is there any cure for depression?'

Counsellor: 'Depression comes in many types and forms, Bill. Research by the experts states that most depression clears up in due course even when untreated, but I'm sure that with God's help you are going to come through this victoriously.' (It's time now to determine whether Bill's depression is physiologically caused, or whether there are psychological or spiritual factors at work here.) 'Tell me, Bill, have you seen your doctor about it and, if so, what did he say?'

Bill: 'Yes, my doctor says it's probably "endogenous" —whatever that means—but he says he can't be quite sure. He did question me a good deal about my habits, my attitude to life, and the way I deal with problems.'

Counsellor: 'Well, that's interesting—interesting that he should say it is "*probably* endogenous". It suggests that although he thinks your depression is arising from some chemical reaction within you—for, roughly speaking, that is what "endogenous" means—it does leave room for the possibility of your depression having another cause.' (Bill still doesn't seem at ease with me. Perhaps I'm too professional in my approach. Maybe I need to listen more and build a stronger bridge of empathy.) 'Tell me, Bill, what are some of the other ways in which this depression affects you?' (If I let Bill talk a bit more, it might help him to relate to me better. I need his trust and confidence if I am to help steer him through this to God's goals for his life.)

Bill: 'Well, it's causing problems in the family. My wife is getting hurt by my sullen moods. The children don't know what's wrong with me. I heard them talking in the bedroom the other night, and one of them said, "What's wrong with Daddy these days? He jumps on us over the slightest thing." I don't mind telling you that made me feel pretty lousy.'

Counsellor: 'I can imagine that, Bill. How is it affecting your work?'

Bill: 'I'm not too bad at work. It seems to lift a bit when I get into the office, but as soon as I leave it settles on me again.'

Counsellor: (I've been listening, asking relevant questions, tuning in to Bill's hurt feelings. It's time now to evaluate his level of need. It's evidently not shock or panic or even a crisis, as Bill seems a fairly responsible person and is coping bravely with the situation. I think it's a predicament. It's not an easy problem to solve, but I am going to trust the Holy Spirit to help me to resolve it. It's time now to let Bill know that I've comprehended his problem and feel for him in it, so I'll reflect back the situation as I see it.) 'Bill, let me see if I understand your problem correctly. For several weeks now you've been feeling depressed. This depression has affected your relationships with your family, and also with God. You find yourself snapping at your children, making molehills into mountains, and no matter how much you pray, you feel as if God is not concerned. Your doctor believes your depression is not chemically caused—that is to say, it doesn't come from a problem in your body. But wherever it comes from, it's making you feel as if you are standing in your own house at night, unable to find the switch to turn on the light because for some reason the switches are no longer there. Is that a fair summary of the situation?'

Bill: 'Yes, that's it—precisely.'

Counsellor: (Looks like at last I'm getting through to Bill. Summarizing it in that way seemed to help him move across the bridge to me. I think he feels I understand his problem so now I'll move on to stage two and find out what Bill is thinking deep down inside himself.) 'Bill, I don't know whether anyone has told you this before, but one of the interesting things about our personalities is the fact that what we think affects the way we feel and how we feel affects the way we act or behave. For example, if I think God doesn't love me then it won't be long before I feel anxious, insecure and threatened in my emotions. Does that make sense?'

Bill: 'I guess I've never thought about it before. But

how is this going to help me with my depression?'

Counsellor: (I've got to go steady here. Bill is getting anxious and wants me to help him change his feelings without going by the biblical route—thoughts affect feelings and feelings affect behaviour. I think I'd better come right to the point now. I believe I've got Bill's confidence. He's in a hurry to find help but I've got to show him the goal I am heading for. I wouldn't normally do this so early but I think Bill is strong enough to accept it.) 'Bill, we are going to get to grips with your depression, believe me, but let's move along a stage at a time. You are a Christian, and I can therefore talk to you as a brother in Christ and man to man. Let me ask you at this stage: what do you expect to happen during our time together?'

Bill: 'Well, I expect these feelings to change—to get rid of my depression and to feel better. Is that too much to ask?'

Counsellor: 'No, it's not too much to ask, Bill. That is precisely what God wants to do for you. He wants you to experience the emotions that are described so beautifully in Galatians 5:22-23. Let me read them for you. "But when the Holy Spirit controls our lives he will produce this kind of fruit in us: love, joy, peace, patience, kindness, goodness, faithfulness, gentleness and self-control..." (TLB). Is that how you would like to feel?'

Bill: 'I'd give the world to feel like that.'

Counsellor: 'Well, that's the way God has designed you to feel. But in order to experience those feelings we have to come along the biblical route which is via our thinking. You say your goal in counselling is to experience a change in your feelings. I can certainly understand that, feeling the way you do, but if we are to find God's answers in this situation we must see what *his* goal is. Let's look at Hebrews 13:15-16: "By him therefore let us offer the sacrifice of praise to God continually, that is, the fruits of our lips giving thanks to his name. But to do good and to communicate forget not: for with such sacrifices God is well pleased." This verse tells us that our major goal in life is to *please God*. Our very existence on this earth is designed by him to bring glory to his name. This is extremely important, Bill, as you will see more clearly later. If you say your goal is to change your feelings then, although I can understand that because of the way you are feeling, the goal you are aiming for is not God's goal. So let's establish God's goal before we go any further, so that we can see it clearly and move towards it. God's goal for each one of us is to please him. We must commit ourselves to doing that *whether we feel like it or not*. My purpose in this counselling session is not primarily to change your feelings, but to help you become more like the Lord. What do you think about what I've just said?'

Bill: 'Well, I must say I feel a little overwhelmed by it all. I'm not sure whether I can honestly commit myself to wanting God's will before my own. At the moment, I'm not as on top spiritually as I used to be, and it's hard for me to make that kind of decision.'

Counsellor: 'I'm not saying it's easy, Bill. God knows how I have struggled with my own self-centredness and wanted my own way when God was showing me all the time that his way is best. There is something in everyone of us that rises up when God challenges us, to say, "I want my own way. I want to work this out the way I think best." But I have found in my own experience, and through talking with others, that God always gives the best to those who decide to take his way. Are you willing, before we go any further, to commit yourself to coming down on God's side and saying to your feelings, "I'm going to side for God, and against you"?'

Bill: 'Putting it that way, I can't do anything else.'

Counsellor: 'It's got to be your own decision, Bill. I can only counsel you. I can't force you to do anything.'

Bill: 'I'm sorry if I'm proving difiicult, but it's hard for me to do.'

Counsellor: 'I know it's hard—I often feel like this myself. But as Christians we must face the fact that God will never ask us to do anything without supplying the strength to do it. If you say, "Yes, Lord, I'll commit myself to doing what you want me to do even though I may not feel like it," then the action of your will is all that God needs. He will do the rest by giving you the strength to do what he asks. Will you do it?'

Bill: 'Yes, I will.'

Counsellor: 'Then say it, Bill, and throw your will on the side of God and his word. Say it now as we sit together in his presence: "I commit myself to doing what God says and asks of me even though I may not feel like it."'

Bill: 'I commit myself to doing what God says and asks of me even though I may not feel like it.'

Counsellor: 'Praise the Lord. You have taken the first step on God's road to the solving of your problem.' (Phew! I'm glad we got through that. Thank you, Father. Now help me as I move ahead.) 'Let's get back to what I was saying a little while ago, Bill, concerning the question of thoughts affecting our feelings. Let's put your thoughts on the table, so to speak, and see what you are really saying to yourself down deep inside you. All of us talk to ourselves in sentences. Sometimes we catch ourselves doing it, but whether we do or not it's a pretty safe assumption that we talk to ourselves all the time, and what we say is important. Tell me some of your thoughts, Bill, the sentences you say to yourself day by day.'

Bill: 'Well, let me see now...one sentence I always catch myself saying is "I give up."'

Counsellor: 'That's what I want to know. What other things do you say to yourself?'

Bill: '"I can't do anything right." "Nobody loves me." "Why should this happen to me?" "Everything goes wrong—just when it looked as if things were going right."'

"Why do I suffer like this?" "I can't do anything right.'"

Counsellor: 'You know, Bill, if I kept saying those things to myself I would finish up depressed too. Can you see now that what you think is largely responsible for the way you feel?'

Bill: 'Yes, that's interesting, isn't it? I never thought about it before, but I suppose you're right. If I keep thinking this way my emotions are going to get the message and react accordingly.'

Counsellor: 'You're putting it better than I am, Bill. It's an interesting insight, isn't it?'

Bill: 'It certainly is.'

Counsellor: (It's time I moved down to stage three now and examined Bill's emotional reaction to find out just which emotion is hurting.) 'Tell me, Bill, how do you really feel about life? What I mean is—do you feel life is unjust, has no meaning, isn't worth the effort... or what?' (If I give Bill some words to hang onto, he will probably give me the clue as to which emotion is hurting.) 'Do you feel bitter against life, guilty about your place in it, or just terribly anxious?'

Bill: 'All three, I suppose.'

Counsellor: 'If you could only choose one, which would it be?'

Bill: 'Er... bitter.'

Counsellor: (Just as I thought. Bill is really resenting God because of what has happened, or what is happening to him, and can't see that God only allows what he can use.) 'Bill, do you feel guilty at all about things?'

Bill: 'What do you mean?'

Counsellor: 'Well, sometimes Christians feel guilty when they are depressed because they know that many other Christians will be saying, "He needs to shake himself out of it and learn to live properly as a Christian ought."'

Bill: 'Yes, I feel guilty about that.'

Counsellor: 'Do you feel anxious?'

Bill: 'All the time.'

Counsellor: 'What about?'

Bill: 'That I won't be able to provide for my family... that things will get worse instead of better... that I might lose my job....'

Counsellor: 'Ever think of committing suicide?'

Bill: 'No. I haven't got that far yet.'

Counsellor: (I'm glad about that. Confirms my diagnosis that Bill is in a predicament and not a crisis. I guess if he said "yes" to that question, I would have to buck up my ideas and get to grips with issues much more quickly.) 'Do you still feel, Bill, that out of those three things I mentioned, bitterness, guilt and anxiety, the strongest emotion is bitterness?'

Bill: 'Yes.'

Counsellor: (Looks like, although all three negative emotions are present, bitterness is the most predominant. I'll move to stage four now, and begin to challenge Bill's wrong basic assumptions. This clue of bitterness and resentment will help me here. I need to challenge his wrong belief about why God lets things happen the way he does.) 'Why do you think you are bitter, Bill?'

Bill: 'Well, it's a pretty awful world we live in, isn't it?'

Counsellor: 'What do you mean?'

Bill: 'Well, tragedies take place every day; cars crash, babies die in cots... the world is a dreadful place.'

Counsellor: 'I know what you mean, but there are an awful lot of good things happening. Do you ever think about that?'

Bill: 'Not really.'

Counsellor: 'You mean your view of life is always this pessimistic?'

Bill: 'I suppose so.'

Counsellor: (Bill looks fairly comfortable and secure with me now, I'll turn up the heat just a little.) 'Tell me, Bill, how do you feel about the negative things that happen to you? Things like illness, irritations, trials, difficulties, problems in the family...?'

Bill: 'I guess I feel such things should not happen to me.'

Counsellor: 'Is there any law that says you must be exempted from the trials and difficulties which fall upon others?'

Bill: 'None that I know of.'

Counsellor: 'Then why do you react in this way?'

Bill: 'I don't know.'

Counsellor: 'What was life like at home when you were a young boy?'

Bill: 'Oh, Dad and Mum were always moaning about the state of the world, and how everything seemed to go wrong.'

Counsellor: 'Tell me more.'

Bill: 'Well, they argued a lot, always seemed to be short of money, and never went to church.'

Counsellor: 'Were they affectionate? I mean, did you ever see them kiss each other, touch each other, or show signs of affection to each other?'

Bill: 'No, never.'

Counsellor: 'Did they ever show you affection?'

Bill: 'Not often.'

Counsellor: 'Did they ever compliment you and congratulate you for things you did well?'

Bill: 'I never remember hearing them congratulate me over anything.'

Counsellor: (Just as I thought. It seems uncanny that many people with serious depression have a history of being brought up in a home where there was little love and affection shown or compliments given. Bill's depression could be a defence against his feelings of worthlessness derived from his childhood. But I must be careful not to pull his defence down...that would do more harm than good.) 'Do you believe God likes you, Bill?'

Bill: 'I believe he loves me—yes.'

Counsellor: 'I didn't ask you that. Do you believe he likes you?'

Bill: 'I don't understand.'

Counsellor: 'Well, it's easy to believe God loves us because the Bible says so. But that truth can be something we merely hold in our intellect, and never let it flow with its warmth into our emotions. We believe it as a basic biblical truth, but we keep it away from the area of our feelings. We call this "intellectualizing"—one of those indigestible words psychologists use. It simply means that we believe something in our heads but never let it get through to our hearts. This is why I asked you if you think God likes you. It looks like you can't conceive that his love can flow right down into your emotions, mingle with your feelings, and give you the warmth and inspiration you need. You can believe he loves you at a distance, but you fail to understand that the Lord wants to put his arms round you and relate to you as an elder brother. This is because the deprivation you experienced in those early years has affected your ability to give and receive love. You feel unsure about yourself, about God and about other people. Deep down inside you are saying to yourself, "Why did God let this happen to me? I should have had more love from others than I have had. Then I would not be this way today."' (I've got to move on to stage five now and come up with some answers, because it's obvious that Bill is ready for it.) 'Is what I am saying making sense, Bill?'

Bill: 'It's making more sense than you will ever know.'

Counsellor: 'Bill, I honestly think your depression is arising from your wrong beliefs about God and about life in general. We are going to have to change those beliefs and bring them more into line with what God says and thinks. This is not going to be easy, because you are an expert at wrong thinking. You've had a whole lifetime to practise it. In fact, you're a professional! Every time you find yourself thinking a wrong thought you are going to

178

have to kick it out and replace it with a biblical one. There are three things I want to give you which I consider to be the keys to solving your problem. The first is this: You must see that according to Romans 8:28-29, God only allows what he can use. He will not allow anything to happen to you that can't be worked out for good, so you can rightly praise him for everything. Now before I give you the second key, let me see if you know how to use the first one. The next time something happens to you which appears to be negative and you find yourself reacting like this, "Oh no, I could have done without this," what are you going to do?'

Bill: 'I'm going to take my stand on God's word, Romans 8:28-29, and say, 'Lord, I praise you for this problem because I believe according to your word you would never allow anything to happen to me unless it can bring benefit to my life and glory to your name.''

Counsellor: 'Terrific! By the way, when a negative thought occurs it's often a good idea to resist it out loud and say something like this: "Get out of my mind, you lying thought. You are a liar because God says otherwise." Then state the text or passage that counters that thought. You see, saying it out loud helps to reduce the frequency of the thoughts coming back again. It is a psychological device which can work towards spiritual ends. Now are you ready for the next key?'

Bill: 'I certainly am. By the way, I'm feeling better already.'

Counsellor: 'Wonderful, but remember we are only a third of the way there yet. The second key is this: God alone can meet your basic personal needs. Right from the moment you were born, you had three basic needs: (1) the need to be loved and to feel secure in that love, (2) the need to see yourself as a person of worth in someone else's eyes, and (3) the need to be significant by contributing to life in a positive way. As every one of us was born of parents who were themselves the products of imperfect parents, our basic needs have never been fully met. We can go through life, as many do, by trying to get other people to meet those needs; our wives, our children, our brothers and sisters in the church, our relatives, our friends. But God has arranged to meet those needs himself—fully and eternally. Once we see that many of our internal struggles arise from the fact that we are being pushed towards meeting our unmet needs in our relationships with other people, and let God meet them, we discover what life is all about. It's about giving to others, not using them to give to us.'

Bill: 'Oh, why didn't somebody tell me this before? All my life I have been using people to meet those needs, when all the time I could have had them met in the Lord.'

Counsellor: 'You're catching on quickly, Bill. Can you see what is happening now? As you think right thoughts, your feelings are beginning to change. Isn't that so?'

Bill: 'It's amazing, isn't it? I would never have believed it, but it makes sense. But is this going to work for me tomorrow when I wake up to face another day?'

Counsellor: 'It's like the medicine or the pills the doctor gives you, Bill. It only works if you take it. Let me share with you, however, the third key: God loves you and has a wonderful plan for your life. Remember what I said about the difference between God loving you and liking you? You must see that the deprived emotions you experienced in childhood left you unable to really know and experience love in the way you should. This means you tend to see God's love in the terms that are abstract—away up there, so to speak. You must learn to see the Lord Jesus Christ as your Elder Brother who loves you so much that he gave himself for you on the cross. Think of it like this. If God, when looking down the telescope of time at the beginning of creation, saw this generation in which you and I live being blown up by hydrogen bombs so that everyone was wiped out except you, then he would still have sent his Son to die for you. To God, you are not just one among many—you are the *only* one. He has saved you and given you a spiritual gift by which you can contribute to the health and growth of his church and express those unique qualities that God has built within you. You see, Bill, a lot of spiritual problems are mixed up with psychological problems. For example, the deprivation you felt as a child is psychological, but it is now affecting your life and is hindering you spiritually. Now, just so that I can be sure you have understood what I am saying, would you like to reflect it back to me in your own words?'

Bill: 'Phew, that's a difficult one... but I'll try. You are saying that because my depression is not caused by anything wrong in my body, it must be coming from my wrong thinking. All my life I have been building up negative thought patterns which still continue even though I am an adult. I must call a halt to these patterns and replace them with more biblical thoughts. So when next they come I call them what they really are—liars—and proceed to think as God thinks about that issue. You are also saying, I believe, that I have resented everything that has happened to me because I couldn't see it as part of God's purposes. From now on, I am to thank God for everything because he will only allow into my life what he can use to benefit me and bring glory to his name. I am also to let God meet my basic needs for security, significance... and what was that other one?'

Counsellor: 'Self-worth.'

Bill: 'Yes, self-worth. Then thirdly, I am to hold on to the truth that God loves me....'

Counsellor: 'But does he *like* you?'

Bill: 'Yes, he likes me....'

Counsellor: 'Hold it there a moment, Bill. I'm glad you said that because you have actually touched something I wanted to say earlier but overlooked for some reason.

When you see that God likes you as well as loves you, then you can really like yourself too. Not in an unhealthy way, such as the Greek mythical figure Narcissus, who looked at his reflection in a stream and fell in love with himself. Self-love is different from love of self. As Christians we can love ourselves in a proper and biblical way, for Jesus said, "love your neighbour as yourself"? Anyway, please continue, Bill...I just wanted to get that point in before it was overlooked again.'

Bill: 'When I see that God loves me and let it flow into my emotions...and that he has a wonderful plan for my life, then I can begin to function as he designed me, with gifts and talents that he has provided. Is that a fairly good summary?'

Counsellor: 'That's excellent, Bill. Let me say just one more word about that last point. Whenever you feel that you don't love the Lord enough, remember that that is not your basic problem—your basic problem is that you don't realize how much God loves you. Our love for him, you see, is the echo of his love for us. The Bible says, "We love,—*because* he first loved us." So if you ever find yourself in that position, just get down on your knees and ask God to show you how much he loves you. We can only love in response to his love.'

Bill: 'I hope I am going to remember all this.'

Counsellor: 'You will. I'm going to ask God to drive these things deeply into your spirit. But before we pray together, let me recapitulate the main thrust of my approach to you in this counselling session. When you consciously practise the truth set out in the Scriptures, that you are going to think and act the way God wants you to irrespective of how you feel, then you can expect God to take care of your feelings and give you those positive emotions we read about earlier in Galatians 5. So what are you going to do tomorrow if you feel depression coming on?'

Bill: 'I'm going to take my wrong thoughts, kick them out, and replace them with God's thoughts.'

Counsellor: 'Fine. And what are you going to do if your feelings don't change?'

Bill: 'I'm going to keep doing it.'

Counsellor: 'Why?'

Bill: 'Because I've committed myself to doing what God wants me to do whether I feel like it or not.'

Counsellor: 'I've come to the end of what I feel God wanted me to say now, Bill. But I want to ask you one more question. Have I convinced you against your will to act and think the way God wants you to?'

Bill: 'Of course not. This is something that is now clear, and I am more than grateful to you for the time you have given me and for presenting God's word to me so challengingly, yet so lovingly.'

Counsellor: (How glad I am for that bit of advice I received in training, that the first thing one has to do in counselling is to show people what they need and then show them how to obtain it. Showing Bill that he has legitimate needs to feel security, significance and self-worth certainly motivated him to reach out to God in this session. I'm thankful I'm a Christian counsellor and not a secular one, because this way I am working with the grain of the universe.) 'Before you go, Bill, let's pray together, shall we?' [Bowing head] 'Father, thank you for bringing my brother Bill here today for counselling. I thank you for upholding him as I brought him those deep challenges to his spirit. Lord, it's obvious that you have had the biggest part in this counselling session and I am grateful to you for it. Be with Bill tonight, and tomorrow, and indeed every day, as he puts into practice the principles I have shared with him. Father, it gives us great comfort to know that though we are now going to separate, we carry with us everywhere we go the presence of our 'wonderful Counsellor', the Lord Jesus Christ. Thank you for what you have done here today. We both give you all the honour, all the praise and all the glory. Amen.'

Bill: 'Amen.'

The counsellor then proceeded to give Bill a list of scriptures to memorize and meditate on. A few days later Bill reported that he was feeling 'heaps better'. After a week had elapsed, and after consultation with his doctor, he left off taking anti-depressant drugs. Within a month he had completely changed, and as he went on to build into his thought life biblical truths and principles, he moved forward into a new dimension of living.

Woe to him who is alone when he falls and
has not another to lift him up.
(Ecclesiastes 4:10 RSV)

SCRIPTURE
FOR USE IN COUNSELLING

Anxiety and worry:	Ps 43:5; Mt 6:31-33; Phil 4:6-7,19; 1 Pet 5:7.
Bereavement & loss:	Deut 31:8; Ps 27:10; Ps 119:50, 92; 2 Cor 6:10.
Comfort & blessing:	Ps 23:4; Lam 3:22-23; Mt 5:4; Mt 11:28-30; Jn 14:16-18; Rom 15:4; 2 Cor 1:3-4; 2 Thess 2:16-17.
Developing confidence:	Ps 27:3; Prov 3:26; 14:26; Is 30:15; Gal 6:9; Eph 3:11-12; Phil 1:6; 4:13; Heb 10:35; 1 Pet 2:9.
Protection from danger:	Ps 23:4; 32:7; 34:7, 17, 19; 91:1-2, 11; 121:7-8.
Fear of death:	Ps 23:4; 116:15; Lam 3:32-33; Rom 14:8; 2 Cor 5:1; Phil 1:21; 1 Thess 5:9-10; 2 Tim 4:7-8; Rev 21:4.
Discipline through difficulties:	Rom 8:28; 2 Cor 4:17; Heb 5:8; 12:7, 11; Rev 3:19.
Disappointment:	Ps 43:5; 55:22; 126:6; Jn 14:27; 2 Cor 4:8-9.
Discouragement:	Josh 1:9; Ps 27:14; 43:5; Jn 14:1, 27;16:33; Heb 4:16; 1 Jn 4:15.
Development of faith:	Rom 4:3; 10:17; Eph 2:8-9; Heb 11:6; 12:2a; Jas 1:3, 5-6; 1 Pet 1:7.
Fear:	Ps 27:1; 56:11; Prov 3:25-26; Is 51:12; Jn 14:27; Rom 8:31; 2 Tim 1:7; 1 Jn 4:18.
Forgiveness of sin:	Ps 32:5; 51:1-19; 103:3; Prov 28:13; Is 1:18; 55:7; Jas 5:15-16; 1 Jn 1:9.
Forgiving others:	Mt 5:44-47; 6:12, 14; Mk 11:25; Eph 4:32; Col 3:13.
Friends & friendship:	Prov 18:24; Mt 22:39; Jn 13:35: 15:13-14; Gal 6:1, 10.
Growing spiritually:	Eph 3:17-19; Col 1:9-11; 3:16; 1 Tim 4:15; 2 Tim 2:15:.1 Pet 2:2; 2 Pet 1:5-8; 3:18.
Guidance:	Ps 32:8; Is 30:21; 58:11; Lk 1:79; Jn 16:13; Jas 1:5.

184

Help & care:	2 Chron 16:9a; Ps 34:7; 37:5, 23-24;91:4; Is 50:9; 54:17; Heb 4:16;13:5-6; 1 Pet 5:7.
Living the Christian life:	Ps 119:11; Jn 15:7; 2 Cor 5:17; Col 2:6; 1 Pet 2:2; 1 Jn 1:7.
Loneliness:	Ps 23; 27:10; Is 41:10; Mt 28:20b; Heb 13:56.
The love of God:	Jn 3:16; 15:9; Rom 5:8; 8:38-39; 1 Jn 3:1.
Obedience:	1 Sam 15:22; Ps 111:10; 119:2; Mt 6:24; Jn 14:15, 21; Jas 2:10; 1 Jn 3:22.
Overcoming temptation:	Is 41:10; Mt 26:41; 1 Cor 10:13; Phil 1:6; 2 Thess 3:3; 2 Pet 2:9.
Peace of mind:	Is 26:3; Jn 14:27; 16:33; Rom 5:1; Phil 4:7; Col 3:15.
Persecution:	Mt 5:10-12; 10:22; Acts 5:41; 9:16; Rom 8:17; 2 Tim 3:12; Heb 11:25; 1 Pet 2:20
Praise & gratitude:	1 Sam 12:24; Ps 34:1; 51:15; 69:30; 107:8; 139:14; Eph 5:20; Heb 13:15.
Provision:	Ps 34:10; 37:3-4; 84:11; Is 58:11; Mt 6:33; Rom 8:32; 2 Cor 8:9; Phil 4:19; 1 Tim 6:17.
Return of Christ:	Mt 24:30-31, 36; Lk 21:36; Acts 1:11; 1 Thess 4:16-18; Tit 2:13; 1 Jn 3:2-3; Rev 1:7.
Sickness & infirmity:	Ps 41:3; 103:3; Mt 4:23; Jn 11:4; Jas 5:15-16.
Sin:	Is 53:6; 59:1-2; Jn 8:34; Rom 3:23; 6:23; Gal 6:7-8.
Sorrow:	Prov 10:22; Is 53:4; Jn 16:22; 2 Cor 6:10; 1 Thess 4:13; Rev 21:4.
Strength:	Deut 33:25; Ps 27:14; 28:7; Is 40:29-31; 2 Cor 12:9; Phil 4:13.
Suffering:	Rom 8:18; 2 Cor 1:5, 7; Phil 1:29; 3:8, 10; 2 Tim 2:12; 1 Pet 2:19; 4:12-13, 16; 5:10.
Temptation:	1 Cor 10:12-13; Heb 2:18; Jas 1:2-3, 12-14; 1 Pet 1:6; 2 Pet 2:9; Jude 24.
Trust:	Ps 5:11; 18:2; 37:5; Prov 3:5-6; Is 12:2.
Victory:	2 Chron 32:8; Rom 8:37; 1 Cor 15:57; 2 Cor 2:14; 1 Jn 5:4; Rev 3:5; 21:7.
Witnessing:	Ps 66:16; Mk 5:19; Lk 24:47-48; Acts 1:8; 4:20.

TERMS EVERY
PEOPLE-HELPER SHOULD KNOW

Adjustment mechanisms: Indirect and unconscious ways of gratifying or compensating for a repressed desire. Such mechanisms are attempts to protect a person's self-concept.

Adolescence: The period through which a child passes in becoming an adult. Usually begins between 10-14 and ends about 17-19.

Aggression This is an attack on an object or an idea which might stand in the way of a person achieving any desired object. It can be either physical or verbal.

Alcoholism: An addiction to alcohol usually associated with anxious, worried, or insecure people.

Ambivalence: A conflicting attitude towards an object or person, consisting of more than one feeling at a time, in which positive and negative feelings are approximately equal. (See Jas 1:8.)

Amnesia: Partial or total loss of memory. There are two causes: 1. Organic, in which the brain is damaged, and 2. Emotional, caused by shock or severe fright.

Anxiety: Apprehension, uneasiness, or worried state over something that is about to happen. Has its main source within the mind, and often leads a person to use defence mechanisms. (Excellent remedy in Phil 4:6-7.)

Aptitude: An inborn potential ability to learn a specific kind of activity. This should not be confused with *achievement*, for the latter is the measure of that which is already learned in a particular field. Aptitude is the measure of *potential*.

Catharsis: The therapeutic 'talking out' of painful ideas with a sympathetic and understanding listener. It is the emotional draining away of material that has been poisoning the mind. (See 1 Jn 1:9.)

Compensation: A state in which a person makes up in some way for a real or imagined deficiency. Often operates at an unconscious level.

Compulsion: A meaningless impulse to do a thing. A person may feel compelled to count the number of steps in a flight of stairs or the cracks in a pavement. Mild compulsions are common, but some serious compulsions are often associated with demonic activity.

Conflict: The stress which arises from incompatible desires or demands. The competition of two or more contradictory impulses producing emotional tension.

Conversion: This psychological term should not be confused with Christian conversion whereby a sinner is transformed, but rather the process by which inner conflicts are passed on through the physical, psychological, or physiological media.

Counselling: The spiritual approach designed to help a person solve a conflict and become adjusted to the spiritual laws designed by God for successful living.

Defensiveness The state of being 'on guard' in which a person tends to show the 'good side' and refrains from opening up concerning deep and intimate matters.

Delusion: A belief out of keeping with reality. Several levels such as (1) Delusions of grandeur, exaggerated ideas of one's importance, (2) Delusions of persecution, in which one is fearful of being singled out for maltreatment. (3) Delusions of reference, in which one wrongly assumes that other people are 'talking about me'.

Denial: A defence mechanism in which a person disowns an unwelcome thought and believes he does not have it, in order to allay anxiety or resolve a conflict. Usually supported by fantasy. Only remedy is confession or owning up to one's faults. (See 1 Jn 1:8-10.)

Depression: Undue sadness or dejection, or a melancholy state in which a person feels worthless and apprehensive. Stems primarily from an inner emotional cause.

Disillusionment: The act of freeing a person from illusion. Often seen in teenagers who are obliged to re-examine things taken for granted in childhood and found to be untrue.

Disorientation: Confusion with regard to time, place, or person. Usually follows shock, a fright, or emotional disturbance.

Displacement: The transfer of an emotional attitude, such as hostility, aroused by one person onto another.

Emotional immaturity: A state in which the person fails to develop normal adult degrees of independence or an inability to maintain equilibrium under stress which normal people meet quite easily. Usually takes the form of childish tantrums, sulking, crying, attention-getting, and so on.

Emotional tension: The state of being emotionally aroused in which the body is kept in an emergency state and not allowed to return to normal.

Empathy: An objective awareness of another person's feelings or behaviour. Differs from sympathy, which is the subjective identification with the feelings or behaviour of another. A counsellor can empathize with a person who has committed sin without necessarily sympathizing (emotionally agreeing).

Extroversion: The state of turning one's interest outward, such as an interest in environment and people other than one's self.

Fantasy: A mental mechanism by which a person faced with a conflict will resort to imagining solutions instead of purposefully working them out. If imagination is used to prepare for action it is good, but if it stops there it becomes a threat to maturity.

Frustration: Thwarting of a need or desire.

Habit: A pattern of activity which, through repetition, becomes automatic.

Hallucination: A sensation which though real to the person concerned has no real outside cause.

Heterosexuality: The normal sexual attraction between a male and a female.

Homosexuality: Inverted sexual orientation between members of the same sex. Homosexual activity (i.e., physical and sexual expression) is firmly forbidden by God. (See Rom 1:24-32.)

Hostility: Feeling of enmity, ill will, or antagonism.

Identification: State in which a person attempts to make himself like another person.

Inferiority complex: Strong feelings of inadequacy or insecurity and a tendency to dwell on and overemphasize the feelings of self-doubt which arise in most people from time to time. Sometimes leads to over-compensation.

Inhibit: To retard, restrain, hold back or prevent a response.

Insecurity: Lack of confidence due to being unsure of the love or support of others.

Insight: An understanding and ability to comprehend the inner nature of things.

Integration: The absence of conflict in which the drives of the personality are organized harmoniously.

Intellectualization: A defence mechanism of the ego in which a person avoids facing a problem by talking about it in a detached and objective manner. Through this mechanism a person may sometimes deceive a counsellor into believing he has no real problems.

Introversion: The state of turning one's interests inward, or preoccupation with self.

Maladjustment: Inability to adjust to laws of life or the spiritual laws of successful Christian living.

Manic depressive: A type of mental disorder in which the person alternates between depression and exaltation. Tends to recur again and again. Manic symptoms are elation, over-talkativeness, rapid ideas, and so on. Depression symptoms are a slowing down of ideas and physical activity.

Masochism: A form of sexual gratification derived from the endurance of physical or mental pain.

Masturbation: Self-stimulation of the sex organs. The feelings of guilt or anxiety that flow from this constitute a major problem in young people.

Obsession: A persistent idea recognized as irrational but which continually intrudes into the conscious mind, and is charged with emotional significance.

Personality: The psychological term differs from the popular use of the word and means the sum total of a person: his attributes, drives, aspirations, inhibitions, interests, aptitudes, and so on.

Phobia: An irrational fear which is usually caused by the displacement of an anxiety from its real object to a substitute.

Projection: A defence mechanism in which the person concerned places the blame for his problems on others, and attributes to them his own unethical desires or impulses. Unwilling to criticize himself, he can then criticize others for the characteristic he has imputed to them. (See Mt 7:1-5 and Rom 2:1-3, 21-23.)

Psychosis: A severe mental disorder characterized by delusions and loss of contact with reality.

Puberty: The beginning of adolescence, usually between 10 and 14 years.

Rationalization: A defence mechanism in which the person imagines a more acceptable reason for doing something. In the fable of the fox and the 'sour grapes' the fox saved face by asserting the grapes were sour when the real reason was that he couldn't reach them.

Reaction formation: A mental mechanism in which a person exhibits and believes he possesses the opposite feelings from those he really has. A father may unconsciously reject his son, but yet do everything to prove his affection on the outward level.

Regression: Reversion to earlier behaviour in an attempt to escape from an unpleasant situation.

Regression: Reversion to earlier behaviour in an attempt to escape from an unpleasant situation.

Rejection: The unconscious withholding of genuine affection and love—usually to a child in which the parents may, on the surface, make an attempt to accept the child, yet harbour inward resentment.

Repression: A way in which a person tends to force into the unconscious mind ideas and impulses which are painful to consider.

Sadism: Pleasure in inflicting pain on another person.

Self-acceptance: Acceptance of the abilities, aptitudes, and values of one's personality. Must not be confused with self-satisfaction, its impostor.

Self-concept: A person's evaluation of, or the picture he holds of, himself.

Self-consciousness: An excessive concern with self—especially with the impression one is making on others.

Self-control: The control of one's emotions, desires and actions. One of the fruits of the Spirit (temperance) in Gal 5:22-23.

Sublimation: The process of diverting unacceptable drives into more acceptable channels.

Suppression: The conscious effort to push unacceptable thoughts from the mind.

Transference: A reaction towards others based on a previous relationship which is carried over unconsciously.

Unconscious: The part or aspect of the mind which acts as a 'safe deposit vault' for past experience.

Withdrawal: Retreat from a conflict or situation in which the person removes himself physically or emotionally so as to avoid conflict.

INDEX

190